RESCUE
YOUR
LoveLife

Changing Those Dumb Attitudes & Behaviors
That Will **Sink** Your Marriage

PERSONAL DISCOVERY GUIDE

DR. HENRY CLOUD
DR. JOHN TOWNSEND

INTEGRITY®
PUBLISHERS
Nashville

TO ALL THOSE COUPLES WHO SEEK TO RESCUE THEIR LOVE LIVES
AND FIND THE CLOSENESS AND PASSION THEY DESIRE

Contents

Acknowledgments

To our literary agent, Sealy Yates, and his associate, Jeana Ledbetter, for their guidance and encouragement throughout the entire writing process.

To the folks at Integrity Publishing—Byron Williamson, president; Joey Paul, publisher; Tom Williams, editor; Rob Birkhead, vice president of marketing; and Angela DePriest, managing editor—for the vision, excitement, creativity, and excellence that have helped make this book a reality.

To our assistant, Janet Williams, for her care and steadfastness in always getting those things done that needed to get done.

To our parents, Henry and Louise Cloud, and Jack and Becky Townsend, for modeling marriage for us for a combined total of well over one hundred years.

To our wives, Tori and Barbi, for their grace, their love, and the many sacrifices they have made to keep our own love lives rescued.

To the staff of Cloud-Townsend Resources, for their dedication, support, and partnership over the years.

To Steve Arterburn and the New Life Ministries gang, for all the diligence and help they bring to us.

To Bill Dallas and Church Communication Network, for their partnership and vision in giving people access to programming that promotes spiritual growth and leadership.

Special thanks from John to couples whose relationships have meant a great deal to me: Tom and Martha McCall, Ted and Jennifer Trubenbach, and Eric and Debbie Heard. You have spoken well into my own life and marriage.

And special thanks from Henry to couples whose relationships have meant a great deal to me: Bill and Julie Jemison, Guy and Christi Owen. You have spoken well into my own life and marriage.

Read This First

If you have picked up this book, there's a good chance that it says two things about you: one, you would like your marriage to be loving, close, and passionate. And two, those things aren't happening in your marriage as they should be.

If that is so, don't give up hope. We are glad you're here, and we want you to know that there is a lot that can be done to rescue your love life! Your marriage is worth rescuing, and this book will show you how that works.

Think back for a moment to the first weeks—maybe months—of your connection with your spouse. What a magnet you guys were for each other! Most likely, you were somewhat obsessed with the other person. You felt strong desires, attractions, tenderness, and depth. You experienced emotions, laughter, and tears. When you were together, it was awesome. Apart, you missed the other.

And then . . . for whatever reason, and there are lots of them, the fire started going out. You saw a part of your mate that you didn't relate to. Maybe someone became withdrawn, self-absorbed, controlling, manipulative, irresponsible—even hurtful. Your communication and connection weren't what they had been during the good times. You began having dumb ideas about the other person, and you two started doing dumb things!

Little problems led to larger ones, and before you knew it, the desires, intimacy, and passions began to wane. In their place came distance, alienation, loss of trust, conflict, a growing numbness, and the fear that this might not ever get better. Now what do I do? Am I stuck here forever?

If this is anything like your journey, don't be discouraged. You're not alone. Many couples have the experience of what happened to that great connection we used to have, and can we ever get it back?

Take the story of Ron and Deb, for example. When they first met and fell in love, they couldn't get enough of each other. It was romantic, passionate, and full of energy and dreams for the future. Their friends envied their happiness.

But, as it happens to so many couples, they started a slow slide into alienation, hurt feelings, and fighting. Problems turned into serious issues. There were less and less good times between them. The honeymoon was definitely over, and the reality wasn't good.

The couple tried all the usual tactics: being more positive, having more date nights, and getting busy with work and parenting. But that just made everything seem worse. Though things looked better on the outside, the two felt fake, empty, and even more distant from each other.

Soon Ron began working longer hours, and spending more time with his buddies. Deb got super-involved with the kids. And the chasm of disconnection became wider and wider, until they saw no way to bridge it. In fact, the slow slide picked up speed, and before they knew it, they were contemplating divorce.

Finally, they were exposed to the principles in this book. They began working the steps. They saw the root causes of the problems they had not been aware of. They learned how they affected each other, and the relationship. They practiced tips and guidelines to resolve issues, heal hurts, and move on toward love and passion. They began opening up again to each other, and, best of all, they recaptured the passion and intimacy they had given up on!

Today, Ron and Deb are again in love with each other and are moving on in their marriage. They have experienced the rescue.

This couple's success story has been experienced by many others who have worked through these principles. The rescue concepts really work and have done so for a long time. It isn't a magic pill, but it is something much better: a proven system of looking at your love life and at yourselves, and learning how to take the steps to make things better. You'll learn how to "unlearn" those dumb ideas that started a lot of this mess in the first place!

Now, suppose the marriage is out of balance, and one of you is more interested in rescuing your love life than the other. Don't give up. There are lots of things you can do, and we will show them to you. You can maximize your own efforts to help bring connection and intimacy to your marriage. As you'll see here, one person can make a huge difference in the relationship.

So get started on your own rescue. We hope and pray the best for your love life!

Suggestions for
Small Group Leaders

One of the most powerful, proven, and effective forces for rescuing a love life is a small group. We thank you for being a facilitator of this effort. We truly believe that you are partnering with us in this adventure of developing strong, intimate, and passionate relationships.

For the rescue effort to succeed, though, the small group needs to be safe, and safety comes when some basic ground rules are observed.

- Things that are discussed need to be held in confidence. No one is to repeat outside the group anything that is shared inside the group.
- The group is not there to solve problems; group members are there to love, encourage, and support one another. Truth and feedback can be very transforming and helpful as long as the group is safe and accepting and all the members are open to receiving feedback. Make sure people offer feedback humbly, relationally, and never in a judgmental or lecturing manner. Members of a small group may also hold one another accountable and benefit from the modeling other people are offering. But no one should ever be made to feel like the target of an extreme makeover!
- Safety also comes with knowing that people will be sharing rather than monopolizing the small-group time. Remind the talkers in the group to give others an opportunity to speak, and encourage the quiet folks to risk sharing a little. That's a growth opportunity for people at both ends of the spectrum!
- That said, encourage and affirm people's participation. Every answer and comment is significant, so listen carefully and show that you're interested in what is said.

- Don't be afraid of moments of silence, especially right after you ask a question. Even if folks have thought through and answered the questions before coming to the meeting, speaking answers out loud in front of a group of people they may not know well is a big step. Realize that waiting ten seconds for someone to speak may feel like an eternity. Sometimes the silence means that someone is thinking deeply or listening to the Holy Spirit.
- Prayer is an important aspect of a small group. If you and/or your group decide to close the meetings with prayer, guard those minutes. You might even want to appoint someone to be timekeeper so that you're sure to end the discussion with time for prayer requests and prayer.

Those general tips apply to any small-group meeting. Now here are some specifics about a *Rescue Your Love Life* small group.

- At the end of each of the eight sections, you'll notice these words of encouragement to small-group members:

> **When you go to the meeting, be ready to . . .**
> - SHARE YOUR ANSWERS TO THE STARRED (★) QUESTIONS.
> - CHOOSE WHICH OF THE LIFELINES YOU'LL GRAB AND WORK ON THIS WEEK.
>
> **During the week . . .**
> - AS YOU WORK ON YOUR LIFELINE, PAY ATTENTION TO THE EFFECTS OF YOUR EFFORTS ON YOU, ON YOUR MATE, AND ON YOUR MARRIAGE.

Valuable small-group time could be spent simply discussing the lifelines small-group members chose to work on and the effect of their efforts on their marriage.

- Another option is to discuss in small groups the three questions in each section that are marked for discussion with a star (★). These questions tend not to be extremely self-revelatory (after all, personal growth and one's marriage are very personal topics), and many of the questions are opportunities for brainstorming solutions to challenges that most, if not all, married couples face.

- You know your group members and how open with one another they are ready and able to be. Also, as the weeks go by, you'll get to know what issues everyone or almost everyone faces. In light of that knowledge, go ahead and choose the questions—marked with a star (★) or not—that will be most beneficial for the people in your group.

- Certain questions along the way might be better addressed by men talking with men, and women with women. Don't hesitate to divide your small group into two smaller groups on occasion.

- Be prepared for pain and emotion to emerge. Offer compassion, your presence, and unconditional love. If issues arise that require professional attention, have available specific information about how a group member can get in touch with competent and known counselors. Be sure to point a believer to the Cross, but avoid Christian platitudes and pat answers. Life is full of pain and loss—as Jesus Himself experienced! Enter into another's pain rather than trying to explain it away or deny its existence.

- Finally, be prepared for God to work in and through your group members. He does amazing acts of freeing and healing, transforming and renewing us when we are open and honest about our hurts, our needs, and our fears—and when we open ourselves to receiving His love through His people.

Blessings on your small-group discussions and prayer time! And let us know how the rescue efforts go! You can contact us at:

Cloud-Townsend Resources
3176 Pullman Street, Suite 105
Costa Mesa, CA 92626
www.cloudtownsend.com
800-676-HOPE (4673)

—Dr. Henry Cloud
—Dr. John Townsend

DUMB ATTITUDE #1

"My Lover Should Make Some Changes"

So why does a book on marriage begin by telling you to change *yourself* first? Because growing marriages are made up of growing people. A relationship is only as good as the two individuals who make it up.

Are you a "growing" person? Explain your answer—and support it with specific evidence from your life.

Why might shining a spotlight on your own issues, baggage, hurts, weaknesses, and faults help your marriage?

What issues, baggage, hurts, weaknesses, and faults come to mind when you think of things you might need to work on?

_____

_____

_____

As you better understand what makes you tick and begin to resolve these matters, your capacity to love, to give grace, to improve communication, to be honest, and to solve problems is greatly enhanced. So starting with yourself is the best way for you to get what you want.

What prompted you to pick up this book? What makes you think you/your marriage needs rescuing in little ways or in big ways?

_____

_____

_____

As you open this book, what hopes and/or goals do you have for your marriage? For yourself?

_____

_____

_____

Even if your mate isn't into dealing with himself, your own example of dealing with yourself and improving your way of relating can profoundly affect the relationship—and your mate—for good and for love. And it is surprising how that can free your mate to begin to rescue himself also.

When, if ever, have you been positively impacted—or at least encouraged—by someone else's positive change and growth?

_____

_____

_____

In this section, we will give you several proven principles that will help you to look at yourself and your own contributions to the relationship. And we will give you guidelines to assist you in applying change and growth to both yourself and to your love life. Let's get started!

> *Lord God, I know that You are the God of the impossible. Nothing is too tough for You to fix or improve; nothing is beyond Your rescue or redemption. You know better than I do the state of my marriage and the condition of our hearts, and it's good to know that everything is in Your care. Right now, Lord, please help me to open my eyes—to want to open my eyes—to my blind spots, my shortcomings, and my sins that aren't helping my marriage. Then, after the self-examination, help me to do the work of adjustment—to want to do the work—that, by Your grace, will make my marriage one that better glorifies You. In Jesus's name. Amen.*

Change Yourself, Not Your Lover

Think about Dennis and Kathleen's story.

What details about their "before" relationship can you identify with?

_____

_____

_____

Which of Kathleen's emotions have you felt? Which of Dennis's thoughts have you had?

_____

_____

_____

Kathleen took action even though Dennis didn't. She explained, "I just started being intimate and more vulnerable with him, taking risks about my feelings and fears and dreams. I poured out my feelings, but without insisting that he do the same. I gradually began to ask him how he felt about things, encouraging him to talk about his feelings. . . . I realized that *whether or not Dennis responded, the steps I was taking were good for both of us.* I wasn't as resentful after that."

★ What do you think about Kathleen's course of action?

_____

_____

_____

What about Kathleen's example might you follow?

_____

_____

_____

_____

What about Dennis' example is instructive?

_____

_____

_____

Start with the Right Focus

Whatever your situation, the best thing you can do right now to rescue your love life is to focus on yourself, not on your lover. As Kathleen discovered, good things can happen to the relationship when you start working on *you*. Changing your own attitudes can do great things for you and your marriage.

Are you up for testing the truth of that statement in your own marriage? Why or why not?

_____

_____

_____

What might be a first step in "working on *you*"?

_____

_____

_____

_____

Health Breeds Health

Just as sit-ups help lower back pain, things you do individually can help your marriage. And generally speaking, *you can do more to improve your relationship than you think*. Let's look at the three key things you can do yourself and bring good light to your connection.

YOU CAN ADD HEALTHY INGREDIENTS TO THE MARRIAGE. Kathleen made herself vulnerable to Dennis instead of resenting and nagging him. By working on herself, she made openness, trust, and safety easier for Dennis; she also got rid of distance, stonewalling, and blame. And her involvement in her small group gave her connection, meaning, and support, which flowed into her marriage.

★ What can you do to make yourself more vulnerable to your mate?

If your mate makes him/herself more vulnerable and open to you, in what way do you want to respond?

YOU CAN INFLUENCE YOUR MATE. Changing yourself helps you to influence your mate to change and grow—and influence is much more effective than any attempt to make your spouse change. That's always an exercise in futility. Instead, you model, give information, make requests, and be vulnerable and safe—and you always respect your spouse's choice.

When, if ever, has someone's influence affected you—your attitudes, your behavior—in a positive way? Be specific about the means of that influence (what did that person say or do?) as well as its impact.

★ Think of an aspect of your spouse that you have tried to change. What might you do to influence growth instead of trying to force it?

YOU CAN RECRUIT YOUR MATE TO HELP YOU. Recruit your mate to the team concept. Have some conversations about what you both want together: more connection, more safety, more emotional intimacy, more vulnerability, more honesty, more authenticity, a greater sense of being a team, and a more satisfying sexual relationship. Also talk about how you affect each other, ways you let each other down, and what you want from each other. Then shoulder the burdens of changing in the right ways.

What evidence can you point to that you're paddling your side of your marriage boat?

Confident that you're working at your marriage, develop a plan for recruiting your mate. Be specific and prayerful as you plan and act.

Love Grows When Dependency Goes

Very often, dependency and love seem to merge as one.

★ What do you see as the difference(s) between dependency and love?

_____

_____

_____

★ Explain why, despite their differences, dependency and love go hand in hand.

_____

_____

_____

There is certainly a kind of need and dependency that two people in love should have with each other, a dependency that is healthy and satisfying. For example, we all need to know our partner will be there with us and for us when we are down and stressed. That kind of dependency is part of support, empathy, and care. But another kind of dependency can smother romantic love. We will show you the difference and give you ways to overcome the dependencies that might be killing your love life.

Love concerns itself with reaching out to another person. At its essence, *love is taking a stand for the benefit of that person* (1 John 4:7). In contrast, *dependency is a state of needing the other person, so that you will become complete and secure.* It is about you more than about the other person. It perceives the other as a need-meeting resource rather than as a person in his own right, with his own viewpoint and needs. Which characterizes your marriage right now: love or dependency? Give supporting evidence.

In what ways, if any, do you think you have a healthy dependency on God? On people? Again, give evidence.

In what ways, if any, do you have an unhealthy dependency on people? Also, who—if anyone—has an unhealthy dependency on you?

Adults do depend on adults, and partners do depend on their partners. But one adult no longer takes primary responsibility for the other. Rather, they walk together as partners in life and growth.

In what way(s) are you and your mate equal companions on this journey of life? Point to signs that each of you is still responsible for his own life, welfare, and health of one's soul instead of being parent to a child.

_____

_____

_____

The Source of the Problem

Though love and dependency are very different, they produce the same result, which can be confusing. *Love and dependency both serve to draw two people together.*

If your dependency is an issue in your marriage, consider the following possible sources:

• Cold, distant, preoccupied, absent, or depressed caretakers who provided only an insufficient amount and quality of love

• Warm and loving relationships with caretakers, but ones in which choice, freedom, and autonomy were discouraged and even punished

• Experiences that taught that being dependent and child-like is good and being a separate individual is not good

• Inconsistent love from caretakers

• Trauma

What will you do to determine the source of your dependency or, if you already have, to deal with that dependency issue?

_____

_____

_____

Dependency in the Love Connection

Several problems can emerge in a relationship in which a partner's dependency has not been resolved.

Which of the following, if any, have you encountered in your marriage?

❏ INABILITY TO LOVE—being unable to love because your concern for survival of self is greater than your concern for the other person or even awareness of his needs

❏ ISSUES OF SEPARATENESS AND DIFFERENCE—resisting being separate and different from your spouse

❏ POWER SHIFTS—giving enormous power to the other person

❏ FREEDOM PROBLEMS—feeling threatened by the other person's freedom

❏ PASSION CONFLICTS—Experiencing problems with sex and romance due to a parent-child connection in the marriage

What will you do about the problem you just identified? We have some suggestions for you below.

_____

_____

_____

Growing Out of Dependency

Below are several keys to success in growing through dependency into secure and happy adulthood.

FIND PLACES FOR DEPENDENCY TO MATURE. Options are a good small group, support group, or counselor.

ENCOURAGE RISK AND AUTONOMY. Affirm and support when the dependent person steps out on her own,

notes:

when she speaks her mind, confronts, gets angry, or does something without you.

CONFRONT THE PATTERNS. Take action when you see the warning signs of dependency, such as "You don't love me anymore" statements, control issues, and resistance to freedom.

STAY OUT OF THE COMFORT ZONE. Address the issue, because your parent-child connection can cause the relationship to become boring, unhealthy, stifling, and controlling.

DON'T BE AFRAID OF NEED. "I need you to be my loving partner/be there for me as I will be for you/help me grow" is a supportive dependency that's good for you. "I need you to survive/be happy/not be lonely/feel good about myself" is problem dependency.

Which key will you focus on first—and what specifically might you do?

_____

_____

_____

A Lifeline: DON'T GET DOWN ON YOURSELF IF YOU HAVE DEPENDENCY PROBLEMS. INSTEAD, REALIZE THAT THE TIME HAS COME TO FINISH THE GROWTH AND MOVE INTO MATURITY—AND ACT. YOU CAN DO IT!

But I'm Not the Immature One

Dave needed to recognize his immaturity. Do you? Most of us

qualify for the label "immature" at some level, and immaturity is another of those dumb things that can sink a marriage. But it's also something we can overcome, and growing out of it can bring closeness, intimacy, and passion.

What Is Immaturity?

To be immature is to be incomplete or undeveloped. In terms of emotional and personal growth, it has to do with certain attitudes that show that an individual has not yet become an adult in the full sense of the word. These attitudes affect one's ability to love, relate, care, and build good relationships.

Look in the mirror. Which of the following indications of immaturity do you see in yourself?

❏ DETACHMENT—the tendency to disconnect from a relationship

❏ CONTROL—resisting your spouse's freedom, expressed through intimidation, aggressiveness, manipulation, or guilt

❏ IRRESPONSIBILITY—being unreliable; not doing what you promise, not taking initiative to solve problems, or not owning up when you make a mistake

❏ SELF-CENTEREDNESS—the inability to step out of your own point of view and enter the world of another's feelings, values, experiences, and opinions

★ What effect has your immaturity had on your marriage?

_____

_____

What Immaturity Does to Your Relationship

As you may have realized firsthand, immaturity causes imbalance, loss of safety and love, and negative feelings in marriage.

In what ways is your spouse partnering with a twelve-year-old?

_____

_____

_____

What grown-up topics do you think you—and therefore your spouse—might be failing to deal with?

_____

_____

_____

Deal with It Now

The one good thing about immaturity is that it's not an incurable disease. The right treatment will get rid of it, and it's something you can do. The sooner you begin, the sooner you will have the kind of love life you really want. Here are some ways to deal with immaturity.

LOOK AT YOUR OWN IMMATURITY FIRST. This is an act of love—taking a step so that your immaturity no longer hurts your spouse and interferes with love. As a couple, you need to agree that whoever does not first look at his own issues is disqualified from judging the other spouse's immaturity.

DETERMINE HOW SEVERE YOUR IMMATURITY IS. How severe is your immaturity? Ask your spouse and other people you trust. Humbly listen to their feedback, remembering that we have a tendency to minimize our effect on others. Start working on the problem.

What If My Spouse Doesn't See His Immaturity?

Take the time and effort to help your mate become aware of how his attitude affects you and the marriage. This can come in the form of certain appeals, requirements, boundaries, and consequences, which are often very helpful in both people getting back on the same page.

A Lifeline: FACING YOUR IMMATURITY IS A MATURE THING TO DO—AND IT'S THE FIRST STEP IN OVERCOMING IT. AND HERE'S ANOTHER: SAY TO YOUR SPOUSE, "I WANT TO TALK ABOUT OUR LOVE LIFE AND HOW TO MAKE IT BETTER. I WANT TO KNOW WHAT YOU FEEL I AM DOING TO CONTRIBUTE TO THE PROBLEMS."

You Make Me Crazy

Sometimes it's obvious that something is wrong in your marriage, but you can't put your finger on what. If you have certain repeating, crazy-making patterns that do not change or resolve over time, that's a sure sign that there's a problem somewhere. We'll show you a way to identify and solve these elusive problems. Let these patterns be a source of diagnostic information, not what sinks your marriage.

Brian and Lori Deal with an Unresolved Issue

As Brian and Lori experienced, if you do not deal with the underlying issue, you can be sure that you will see it again. So they dealt with what was going on underneath their inability to solve problems and handle conflict well.

★ What did you learn from Brian and Lori's situation?

_____

_____

_____

What recurring pattern in your marriage needs attention?

_____

_____

_____

Dealing with emotional baggage that has not been resolved is a major key to rescuing your love life. All the good intentions, date nights, and positive affirmations in the world won't deal with or get rid of an issue. The patterns will continue until you face the problem and apply the solution.

Many Causes, Many Patterns

There is not enough room in this workbook to list all the issues that can cause negative patterns in a marriage. But here are a few of the common ones—and all are fixable.

Which of the following issue(s) may be behind negative patterns in your marriage?

❏ TRUST ISSUES—having trouble opening up and being vulnerable

❏ RESCUING—enabling bad behavior and attitudes in others by rescuing them from the results of their bad behavior instead of confronting the issues themselves

❏ PASSIVITY—not taking initiative, avoiding conflicts

❏ LACK OF INTEGRATION—being unable to see others as both good _and_ bad, and being unable to live in that reality

The list could go on and on. The point here is to remember that often, *the recurring pattern is not the problem*. It is more often the symptom of another unresolved issue.

Address Your Issues

Here are a few suggestions that will help you confront and overcome the underlying issues in your marriage.

OBSERVE THE PATTERNS OBJECTIVELY. You are the surgeons; the marriage is on the table. What will you and your spouse do and say to remember—and remind each other—that you're on the same team working on the marriage and trying to diagnose the real disease?

TALK ABOUT WHAT PATTERNS ARE REPEATED. Identify the patterns you and your partner enter into.

OWN WHATEVER YOU ARE DOING THAT KEEPS THE PATTERN GOING. Realize your contribution to the pattern. If you are not aware of your issue, ask your spouse to pinpoint what you are doing. Be humble and listen.

Marriages that truly succeed are marked by this attitude: *each spouse is more concerned about how his own issues affect the love than about his spouse's issues*. Both are determined to look at themselves without excuse or blame. There is no limit to what a marriage that takes this approach can accomplish.

ENTER THE PATH OF GROWTH TO MAKE SURE THE ISSUES ARE RESOLVED. Work on your issues with love, communication, and positive attitudes. Have you tried those? Here are other things to try: Ask your spouse for help and support. Have her remind you when you inadvertently repeat the behavior. Read about it, pray about it, and ask people you know for help and wisdom.

BE AWARE OF REPEATED PATTERNS. Awareness of these patterns lets you know your progress. As the pattern of withdrawal, anger, distance, or anxiety goes away, it shows that you are improving your issues. If the pattern is not going away, either you are addressing the wrong cause or one of you is disengaging from the process. If the pattern is getting better but remains a problem, ask a wise friend what you might be missing.

A Lifeline: Root out the problems underlying the repeated patterns in your marriage. When you resolve the issue, you should see great change and progress.

One Person Can't Change Everything, But . . .

Think about Glenn and Nancy's classic detached husband–nagging wife situation.

In what ways, if any, is their relationship similar to yours? Be specific.

_____

_____

_____

★What did you think about Nancy's course of action? Wives, would you have been able to take those risky, courageous steps? Explain.

_____

_____

_____

★ Share your reaction to this couple's happy ending. Husbands, can you imagine experiencing the change of heart that Glenn did? Why or why not?

_____

_____

It wasn't easy for Glenn to get out of his detached comfort zone and connect with Nancy, but with her encouragement, he moved out of the cocoon. They now have a much better relationship. She helped transform her marriage with an unwilling husband, and that helped him become a willing partner in growth.

One Is Almost a Majority

You may have a partner who is unwilling to deal with a problem, but there is a lot you can do all by yourself to help and change.

First, identify the problem. What problem is your partner unwilling to deal with? Is it a problem of connection, as with Glenn and Nancy, or a problem with irresponsibility, selfishness, or some other bad attitude or behavior?

_____

_____

What have you contributed or do you contribute to this problem? Remember that Nancy was definitely not helping the situation, so be honest with yourself as you look at your own situation.

_____

_____

You may feel helpless and alone in your marriage. You may be thinking, *Nothing can change until my partner wants to change.* Fortunately, that is not true at all. You don't have to wait until your lover is ready to get moving. There are some moves you can make to help him get moving.

Explain chaos theory (Book pg. 33) **in your own words.**

_____

_____

_____

★ **What encouragement do chaos theory and the butterfly effect offer you as you think about your connection with your mate? Be specific.**

_____

_____

_____

As one person makes changes, those changes affect the partner in some way, because your lives are connected. If one person changes, the relationship changes.

Nancy didn't try to control Glenn. She changed her patterns in a healthy way that didn't work against the relationship. But her changes affected him, and he responded. What healthy changes in your patterns could you make? Be careful not to work against the relationship—and be sure that you have enough connection to handle whatever step you take.

_____

_____

_____

Basically, the chaos theory says that you must not give in to hopelessness and helplessness because *you can affect things.* As you bring light, love, truth, and health to the relationship, it exposes problems and helps make changes (Ephesians 5:13–14).

How One Can Do a Lot

Here are some ways you alone can make good changes that can do a great deal to resolve your relationship conflict in positive ways.

SAY WHAT YOU WANT AND NEED. Be clear and specific about what you need that will help end the problem.

What do you need? (See the possibilities on Book pgs. 33-34.)

_____

_____

_____

Does your partner know what you need? If you think so, when did you tell him—or are you equating love with clairvoyance and expecting him to know what you need? Or are you being too global in your statements?

_____

_____

_____

Educate your partner about what you need, and be clear, direct, and specific. Plan your words right now—what will you say?

_____

_____

_____

SAY WHAT IS NOT OK. If you don't draw a line, your partner has a point when she says she never knew that she crossed it.

Does your partner know specifically what attitudes and behaviors hurt you, bother you, distance you, and will no longer be tolerated by you? (See the possibilities on Book pg. 34.) What is not OK?

_____

_____

_____

_____

With what words will you clearly, directly, and specifically bring these not-OK attitudes and behaviors into the light?

_____

_____

_____

OWN YOUR TRIGGERS. Your reactions are your own reactions. Your partner may certainly affect and influence you, but he doesn't dictate or control how you feel and react.

Comment on this truth—and share what reactions (over-reactions?) of yours come to mind.

_____

_____

_____

What will you do to own or take responsibility for your triggers? What will you say to your mate about your extreme reactions?

Whatever the cause of your emotional reactions, if you blame them on your partner, you force him to defend himself rather than focusing on the problem. Instead, face the problem. Own that you do have extreme reactions to that problem, acknowledge that those extreme reactions aren't his fault, and get moving. How will you do that today?

INITIATE SOLUTIONS. One person can make a great difference in resolving conflict by coming up with ideas, suggestions, and solutions. So take the initiative and be positive.

What will your first problem-solving step be? Will you do research, talk to a professional, or something else?

★ Once you've come up with some ideas or a possible plan, practice sharing your thoughts by completing this statement: "I have a couple of ideas of how we can deal with our conflict . . ." You may not come up with the perfect idea, or even a good idea, on your own. And that's OK. Taking positive initiative in problem solving gets both of you thinking and moving.

BE THE HEALTHIEST PERSON YOU CAN BE. Grow personally, emotionally, and spiritually. Get to know yourself, God, and others in ways that transform and change you. Become loving, caring, defined, honest, responsible, and humble.

What specific step does each of those three instructions suggest to you?

· Grow personally, emotionally, and spiritually.

· Get to know yourself, God, and others in ways that transform and change you.

· Become loving, caring, defined, honest, responsible, and humble.

A healthy person inspires a very strong incentive for the other to change. Being a growing individual, a person living in the light, will help your partner get off the fence. It forces him either to become a person of light or to move against the light. Either way, you are better off.

A Lifeline: TAKE ADVANTAGE OF THE TREMENDOUS POWER AND EFFECT YOU HAVE IN YOUR RELATIONSHIP, AND BE AN AGENT FOR CHANGE AND REDEMPTION. ULTIMATELY, YOU CAN BE ON YOUR WAY TO MOVING PAST CONFLICT INTO LOVE, RECONNECTION, AND INTIMACY.

Living What I Learn

Which of this section's six chapters did you find most relevant? Explain.

❏ Change Yourself, Not Your Lover
❏ Love Grows When Dependency Goes
❏ But I'm Not the Immature One
❏ You Make Me Crazy
❏ One Person Can't Change Everything, But . . .

_____

_____

_____

★ Share one or two insights from the text that you found especially encouraging.

_____

_____

_____

Which lifeline will you grab this week?

❏ Work on yourself first, and expect good things to happen!

❏ Realize that the time has come to finish the growth and move into maturity—and act.

❏ Facing your immaturity is a mature thing to do—and it's the first step in overcoming it.

❏ Root out the problems underlying the repeated patterns in your marriage.

❏ Take advantage of the tremendous power and effect you have in your relationship, and be an agent for change and redemption.

What specific steps will you take to help rescue yourself and thereby rescue your marriage?

_____

_____

_____

Who, if anyone, will hold you accountable in your efforts
to rescue your marriage?

_____

_____

_____

As you close in prayer, ask the Lord to help you see yourself as you are so that you can cooperate with the transforming work of His Holy Spirit. Also ask Him to give you the humility and boldness you need to rescue yourself for the sake of your marriage.

When you go to the meeting, be ready to . . .
- SHARE YOUR ANSWERS TO THE STARRED (★) QUESTIONS.
- CHOOSE WHICH OF THE FIVE LIFELINES YOU'LL GRAB AND WORK ON THIS WEEK.

During the week . . .
- AS YOU WORK ON YOUR SECTION 1 LIFELINE, PAY ATTENTION TO THE EFFECTS OF YOUR EFFORTS ON YOU, ON YOUR MATE, AND ON YOUR MARRIAGE.

DUMB ATTITUDE #2

"My Lover Should Make Me Happy"

From the time children watch their first animated movie with a prince and a princess, they begin forming ideas of what love and romance look like. Girls think that someday a knight in shining armor riding a white horse will come for her, and his unfaltering devotion will make her happy for the rest of her life. Guys think that someday he will rescue a damsel in distress, and her unparalleled beauty and passion will make him the happiest man on earth.

★ What ideas (read "childhood fantasies") about love and romance did you acquire from movies, television, and books as you were growing up? Give two or three examples.

_____

_____

_____

_____

As any marriage counselor will tell you, some of the expectations and demands that adult couples have for each other are pretty lofty as well. What expectations and demands of your lover do you make—verbally or nonverbally? (If you're not sure, consider asking!)

_____

_____

_____

If you are willing to get out of the storybooks and into the real world, you can find lasting, fulfilling, and even intoxicating love. Join us as we take a look at how that kind of love is only found in the real world of real expectations. You may even find out that you have not been expecting enough!

Lord God, reality and fantasy are definitely two different worlds, and I may be straddling both. Please show me the ways I am still living in a world of childhood fantasies as well as any unrealistic demands I am making of my lover. Help me be a humble and attentive student as I learn in this section how to let go of those unfair, unhealthy, and unhelpful expectations and how to live in the real world where lasting, fulfilling, and even intoxicating love exists. (I believe; help my unbelief!) In Jesus's name. Amen.

The Real Scoop About Happiness

Denise realized that her failure to be happy was her own problem.

Is that idea new to you? If so, what led you to think otherwise, to think—and live—as if it's another person's job to make you happy?

If you've already realized that your failure to be happy is your own problem, what situation or experience led you to that conclusion—and what have you done as a result?

The Fantasy of Marriage

Here's the dumb attitude in a nutshell: *my spouse should make me happy*. The converse of that idea is this: *my spouse is the reason I am not happy*. The truth is that your happiness is your problem—and also your opportunity.

★ Why do many of us enter marriage with the very popular dumb attitude that our spouse should make us happy?

Why is it so easy to gravitate toward the dumb attitude's corollary that our spouse is the reason we're not happy?

Be honest: to what degree do you have either dumb attitude today?

_____

_____

_____

The Secret of Happiness

First of all, happiness is not a good life goal. A much better life goal is *growth*, and a by-product of growth is happiness.

The spiritual and emotional growth process, designed by God, is about discovering what we lack inside, where we are empty, and where we are broken. We find out how unfinished we are and how much we need God and others. What sense do you have of how unfinished you are? What indications have you seen that you need God and others? Be specific.

_____

_____

_____

This God-designed growth process doesn't stop with our recognition of how unfinished we are. The next step is experiencing the many ways we can be filled, matured, and healed. When, if ever, has God met you at this point of recognition and offered filling, maturing, or healing? Let that experience be an encouragement to you right now. And if you haven't yet experienced that touch of grace, know that God wants you to.

_____

_____

_____

Placing Growth Before Marriage

Let's get the pressure off the marriage! Don't ask from marriage what only personal growth can provide. You will never move from an unloved to a loved state, or from a weak to a strong state, simply from having the right spouse. So let's put the pressure on growing out of whatever is keeping you from being the fulfilled and complete person you need to be. The end result is your marriage, freed from a burden it cannot bear, can become a wonderful haven of love, connection, intimacy, and passion.

First, ask yourself—and this is not necessarily an easy question to answer quickly—what you are demanding from your marriage that you should be achieving in the growth process. Consider these possibilities: You tend to feel empty and unloved. You depend on your spouse to give you a sense of purpose and strength. You hope your mate will add structure and confidence to your life.

Purpose and strength come when we learn what we want, work through why we have been afraid to go after what we want, and then take the necessary risks to achieve it. Spend some time trying to determine both what you want from life and why you have been afraid to go after it. Prayer and conversation with a good friend who's known you long or knows you well may help.

Growth Within Marriage

Another benefit of taking the pressure off the marriage and pursuing your own growth is that *growing people tend to be attractive people.*

Who, if anyone, comes to mind when you think of a "growing" person—and what do you find especially attractive about him or her?

_____

_____

_____

When a person becomes compassionate, she can show compassion to her spouse. When she becomes honest, she can give and receive truth with her spouse. When she has hope for change, she can give that hope to him. When she has experienced that it is OK to be real and imperfect, she can accept reality and imperfection in him. When she can look into deeper parts of her own soul, she can help make it safe for him to reveal his deeper self to her.

Which one of these growth areas will you make top priority? What will you do to move toward becoming more compassionate, more honest, more hopeful for change, more accepting of your imperfections, or more able to look into the deeper parts of your soul?

_____

_____

_____

_____

How to Start a Growing Marriage

Here are some ways to begin the process of rescuing your love life from the dumb attitude that makes your spouse responsible for your happiness.

ASK EACH OTHER IF THE MARRIAGE IS BURDENED WITH THE "HAPPINESS FANTASY." Is one of you expecting the other to make him happy and fulfilled? Also, is one of you blaming the other for her unhappiness? If the "happiness fantasy" is alive and well in your marriage, agree together that the fantasy must die so that real love can live.

COMMIT YOURSELVES TO THE GROWTH PROCESS. As a couple, decide that you will both find ways to deal with your own emptiness and unhappiness.

What setting and context would best foster your growth together? Together, for instance, explore small-group options.

_____

_____

_____

What setting and context would best foster your personal growth?

_____

_____

_____

What commitments might have to change so that you allow time and have energy to work on your marriage?

_____

_____

_____

BECOME COMPANIONS TO EACH OTHER'S GROWTH. The best attitude couples can take is that of two companions: *I will support your growth, and you will support mine. We are not responsible for each other's growth process, but we will help and encourage each other in it.*

★ If your spouse is working on personal growth, what can you do to encourage him?

_____

_____

_____

★ If your spouse is not yet working on personal growth, what can you do to support him nevertheless? (Remember, your nagging will not be as effective as your growth!)

_____

_____

_____

 A Lifeline: KISS THE FANTASY OF THE PERFECT MARRIAGE GOOD-BYE, WITH EACH MATE POURING ECSTASY AND COMPLETENESS INTO THE OTHER, AND TAKE OWNERSHIP OF YOUR OWN HAPPINESS.

Are They Needs or Desires?

Think about Ally and Ben's relationship.

★ What, if anything, about their struggle reminded you of challenges you face in your own marriage?

_____

_____

One of the most important things that partners in a relationship must do is to work hard on expressing, understanding, and meeting the needs of each other.

What have you learned since getting married about understanding and meeting your partner's needs? Give one example.

_____

_____

_____

What have you learned from your marriage about the importance of expressing your own needs?

_____

_____

_____

Expressing your needs may not yet be easy for you, but keep working on it. And as you do, be sure that the things you're defining as "needs" really are needs and not just wishes.

Interpreting wishes as needs is another common but dumb attitude that can sink a love life. But rescue is fairly simple if you know what to do. It's a matter of getting straight about what is a true need and what is not.

Needs, Preferences, and Wishes

What does one truly need in a marriage? *A true need is something that, if missing, results in damage.* If a genuine need isn't met, destruction occurs. Wishes and preferences are great, but we can live without them and not suffer any injury. For example, when I go to a restaurant, I *need* food. I *wish* for pizza on the menu. I *prefer* to sit in a booth.

Mature people make sure their needs are taken care of, and they also try hard to find what they wish for and prefer. Who in your life offers clear evidence that living like this is key to happiness? When they don't get what they want, they are undoubtedly still grateful for the basics.

In marriage, a loving, honest, and responsible spouse is someone to be grateful for. But Ally felt entitled to more than that. What, if anything, do you feel entitled to from your spouse that he is not or cannot give you?

One of the biggest tragedies today is that people feel entitled to have their wishes met. When that does not happen, they feel victimized and shortchanged, like they somehow deserve more than they are getting. So they either get angry with spouses they should appreciate, or they believe the lie and leave to find the fulfillment they feel entitled to.

This "entitled fulfillment" may be physical, romantic, financial, status, lifestyle, intellectual, spiritual, material, social, educational, or other categories. Which of these categories, if any, do you feel your spouse should fulfill for you—but isn't?

Remember the definition of "needs"? If needs aren't met, damage follows. So are these categories of fulfillment genuine needs? Will you suffer damage without them?

What Are Our True Needs?

If you focus on the true needs of your relationship first, you can pursue those other areas of fulfillment as extra benefits, for you and your partner will have the kind of connection that enables both of you to grow to greater heights. What are those needs? Here are the ones we have found.

EMOTIONAL CONNECTION. Empathy, support, care, listening, understanding, bonding, trust, and depending are all parts of what creates an emotional connection. It is the sense of being present with each other in a way that ends isolation, alienation, and aloneness.

FREEDOM. Where there is control, manipulation, or an inability to have an identity apart from the partner, love dies. You have a real need to set each other free from any and all kinds of control. Respect each other's limits. Enjoy each other's individuality and differences. A good relationship serves not only the needs of the relationship but also the individual needs of each partner.

FORGIVENESS. Dare we say it? All of us are sinners. If a relationship is not strong enough to handle sin and failure, then it's not strong enough to handle reality. Our sin and failure create a huge need for forgiveness. If you punish each other for failure and do not forgive, your relationship will suffer damage and die.

ACCEPTANCE. Similar to our need for forgiveness is our need to be accepted regardless of our imperfections. For intimacy and love to occur, we need to reveal our true, naked selves. We'll do that only when we have the assurance of being totally accepted.

LIMITS. In a marriage, limits are essential to keeping love alive. A good relationship does not allow hurtful behaviors to gain more ground, because these negative behaviors destroy love. Express limits and let each other know when something wrong is happening. And speak about it in love.

SECURITY. We need to know that our partner's love is not going away. For love to grow, we need to know that our spouse's love is secure, unconditional, and forever. A secure commitment, one that preserves the connection through all sorts of times, is essential.

EQUALITY AND MUTUAL RESPECT. Romantic love is based on mutual respect and equality, on valuing the contributions, talents, ideas, gifts, perspectives, and uniqueness of each other. Each partner is seen as equally valuable and is treated that way. In such a connection, both spouses become more of who they are supposed to be. This mutuality shows itself in front of others in the form of validation and respect instead of criticism and put-downs.

DESIREDNESS. In your marriage, it is important that each of you communicates your desire for the other. Learn what causes your partner to feel desired, and then act on what you learn.

PHYSICAL EXPRESSION. Humans need to be touched, hugged, caressed, and nurtured physically. Desire, equality, security, and acceptance are all expressed through physical contact. In addition to normal human touch, marriage needs a fulfilling sexual relationship as well, and sex is to be respectful, mutual, accepting, desirous, secure, and free.

TIME. It takes time to develop love, to develop maturity, and to grow a relationship. For you to get all of these needs met in increasing measure, an investment of time is essential.

★ Which of the items on this list surprised you?

Which of your lover's needs are you adequately meeting? (If you're not sure, ask!)

Which of your lover's needs would you do well to invest more time and energy in meeting? (Again, if you're not sure, ask.)

★ If your spouse asks about how well he is meeting your needs, what will you say? Think ahead so that you will speak the truth in love.

Keep the Important Things Important

We want our marriages to meet not only our real needs but also our every expectation, preference, and desire. Demanding that our wishes and preferences be fulfilled is a dumb attitude that will sink a marriage. However, at the same time, we must realize that some needs are truly essential. If these real needs are not met, a relationship will suffer.

"Don't get caught up in fighting about your wishes." Is that advice you need to hear right now? Why or why not?

_____

_____

_____

"Do get caught up in focusing on your needs." Again, is that advice you need to hear right now? Why or why not?

_____

_____

_____

What might you do to learn to better communicate your real needs, educate each other about them, meet them, stand up for them, nurture them, and grow in your mutual ability to meet them?

_____

_____

The ten genuine needs (listed on Book pgs. 46-49) are the things in your relationship worth fighting _for_, not _about_. "If you fight _about_ these needs, you are probably violating one of them. But when you fight _for_ them, you get closer to having them met." What insight does this diagnosis of certain marital conflicts—perhaps some in your own relationship—provide you?

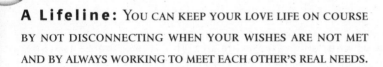

A Lifeline: You can keep your love life on course by not disconnecting when your wishes are not met and by always working to meet each other's real needs.

Stop Looking for Your Other Half

Faith was very excited about her fiancé, Daniel, but she was confused when it came to the mathematics of the relationship. One-half of a person plus one-half of a person does not equal a whole person, much less two whole people! When two incomplete people marry in hopes that merging their strengths will make up for each other's weaknesses, the result is not the happiness they hope for. In fact, what happens is that each partner slowly comes to want from the other the things that that person does not possess. And they begin to tear each other down. They no longer love the attributes that first attracted them. In fact, they now resent them.

What insight into the dynamics of your own marriage did you gain, if any, from the profile of Faith and Daniel's relationship during their engagement? What did you learn from the forecast of what the married future might hold for them?

What strengths in your mate were traits you did not possess when you first fell in love and then married?

Which of your own strengths did you think compensated for your mate's weaknesses or lacks?

Have you come to want from your mate these very traits (ones you mentioned in your answer above) which he doesn't possess? What are you going to do about that?

Do the Relational Math

Looking to your spouse for the strengths and the traits that you lack is another dumb attitude that can sink your marriage. To remedy this very fixable situation, first understand the wrong expectations that are set up in the faulty math problem.

Relationships are not additive, but multiplicative; and when you multiply one-half of a person times one-half of a person (which is the equation in every relationship, since none of us is totally whole), you get one-quarter of a person. That's less than you started with!

Couples who demand that the other "half" display more than the original half that he or she brought to the relationship bring each other down. As is often said, they are attracted to someone because of a certain trait, and then fight about that trait for the next forty years. In what area(s) of your relationship, if any, are you living out this adage?

_____

_____

_____

The key to breaking that pattern or blocking any tendency for it to appear in your marriage is realizing that *everyone* is incomplete, including you and your lover. Your first task is to lower your expectations for that "half-baked" person to be "done." Realize that your mate is still in the oven and that God is at work making him into the complete person that both you and God desire him to be.

Is it difficult for you to accept the fact that you and your mate are not yet fully complete, well-rounded people? Why or why not?

_____

_____

_____

Hints for Living with a "Half-Baked" Person

Give up the demand that your mate be other than he is at this point, and start dealing with it in a better way. What does that mean? Here are some hints on living with a half-baked person—and how you can overcome being one.

ACCEPT YOUR SPOUSE AS AN INCOMPLETE PERSON, JUST AS GOD HAS ACCEPTED YOU. And accept that reality *lovingly*. Stop protesting with rage, nagging, shame, condemnation, and any other way that you do not like to be treated yourself.

LOOK AT AREAS WHERE YOU ARE INCOMPLETE BEFORE FOCUSING ON YOUR MATE'S INCOMPLETE-NESS. Get the plank out of your own eye first (Matthew 7:5). Ask your partner where you need to develop more. Ask what incomplete areas of your personality affect him the most, and begin there. Be a model for change.

BECOME SUPPORTIVE CHANGE AGENTS FOR EACH OTHER IN THE AREAS OF GROWTH YOU NEED. Talk about those things together, not with nagging or judgment, but as teammates. Create a safe space in which you can talk about them in love—no judgment, no shame, no guilt, no anger allowed.

FOCUS ON THE THINGS THAT ARE IMPORTANT FIRST. Address each other's real needs, as we discussed previously. Helping each other grow to completeness in those areas is more important than the stuff you may tend to fight over.

BE PATIENT. This is important: be patient with your partner just as God is patient with you. Want to see how it works? Think of your most incomplete issue as a person (such as procrastination, emotional vulnerability, completing tasks, sharing feelings, or being assertive). How long have you been aware of that issue? How long have you been working on it? How long has God been patient with you? How has He loved you unconditionally along the way? That is the way you have to look at this issue in your partner.

Having read these five points, what change(s) in your attitude would you like to make? Be specific.

_____

_____

_____

In light of these five points, what change(s) in behavior might it be wise for you to make?

_____

_____

What insight into humans and relationships found in these five points is most helpful to you?

_____

_____

Don't Push the Process

You cannot expect your relationship to change overnight. You *can* expect your spouse to hear you and face the problem, but you can't expect immediate maturity. Accept what the marriage is, work on it lovingly, and give each other time to grow.

A Lifeline: TO PRESERVE THE CONNECTION BETWEEN YOU AND YOUR SPOUSE, TWO HALF-BAKED PEOPLE, BE SURE THE RIGHT INGREDIENTS ARE IN THE MIX—LOVE, HONESTY, SUPPORT, FEEDBACK, AND BECOMING WHOLE YOURSELF. SET THE TIMER CORRECTLY FOR MATURITY, GIVING YOUR MATE TIME TO LEARN AND GROW. KNOWING THAT YOU BOTH ARE STILL COOKING, YOU CAN FACE ISSUES WITHOUT POISONING THE CONNECTION THAT WILL BE NEEDED TO HELP YOU BOTH BECOME "FULLY BAKED."

Self-Denial? You're Joking, Right?

Remember the days of being single and having the freedom to do what you wanted, when you wanted? Your schedule, money, friendships, and habits were all yours. You answered to yourself, and that was pretty much it. Then you fell in love and suddenly found yourself having to say no to yourself with respect to freedoms, choices, and preferences you had enjoyed in your previous life. Considering someone else's feelings and desires can be a painful way of having to live life. This way of life is called self-denial.

Think back over the past few days and give three or four examples of saying no to yourself, of not doing what you wanted when you wanted.

_____

_____

_____

Have such acts of self-denial gotten easier since you were first married? Why or why not? Share your thoughts.

_____

_____

_____

★ Self-denial may indeed be painful, but it is literally your only hope of connecting at the deep, intimate, and passionate levels you have wanted and waited for. Why do you think that's the case?

_____

_____

_____

Simply put, self-denial is *the practice of postponing, or even giving up, activities and attitudes that block love and connection.* In healthy marriages, self-denial is a daily way of living, relating, and thinking. And it is one of the most important keys to love.

Contrary to Our Intuition

On an intuitive level, what we just said may not make sense. Isn't love about feeling better inside—more fulfilled, more connected, more encouraged, more energetic? That is certainly one aspect of love and relationship. Love is indeed a transfer of grace, acceptance, comfort, and empathy between two people.

What grace, acceptance, comfort, and empathy have you received from your lover this week? Offer a specific example or two.

_____

_____

_____

What grace, acceptance, comfort, and empathy have you extended to your lover this week? Again, offer a specific example or two.

_____

_____

_____

★ Grace, acceptance, comfort, and empathy offer only part of the entire story of love. It is love at a beginner's level, an immature form. Why is this a good beginning?

_____

_____

_____

True lovers don't expect giving and receiving to be an easy, uncomplicated flow between two people. That is just not reality. The relationship becomes complex as you become aware that you are two separate and different people, and this brings conflict. The two of you have varying viewpoints, wants, needs, desires, values, and feelings. Which of your lover's viewpoints, wants, needs, desires, values, and feelings are different from yours? Give a few specific examples.

_____

_____

_____

Complexity and conflict don't mean that your love isn't the genuine article. Keep reading!

Shut Down the iPod

Consider this simple idea: *self-denial creates the space you both need for love to grow.* The more you understand healthy self-denial, the more you will truly love and give to your mate. And don't be surprised when your lover responds in kind!

★ Remember the iPod analogy (Book pg. 56)? What did that help you understand about healthy self-denial?

_____

_____

_____

Self-denial is the mechanism that helps you shut down the iPod. It allows you to say no, sometimes temporarily and sometimes permanently, to things you are focusing on— your own feelings, opinions, dreams, hurts, needs, and wants. Self-denial helps you make room for the other person's world. Now how are you feeling about self-denial?

When couples learn to deny themselves, they experience a wonderful and transcendent mystery of love: *when I deny "me," I connect with "us."* What taste, if any, of this new level of life—the life of us—have you experienced?

The life of "us" is far superior to the life of "me." "I" serves "we" and is the better for it. Imagine being married to someone who says, "I have decided to let the extra money go for something you want. I just feel like letting you have something good." You cannot help but feel trusting and open to a partner who denies himself. What opportunity for self-denial, for choosing to serve "we," do you currently face?

Don't be afraid to shut down your iPod on your desire and sacrifice it for a greater good. I (John) know that my wife's act of self-denial so that my sons and I could have a music room has brought us much closer, because it caused me to feel much gratitude and love for her.

Having a Self to Deny

Certainly in some connections the love is in trouble because one person gives too much and gets too little. But the more common problem in self-denial is not having enough of a "self" to deny. That is, the one who gives too much (generally, this is more rescuing and enabling than true wholehearted giving) is doing so because she does not yet possess the love and internal structure she needs before she denies herself.

> Do you possess the love and internal structure you need before you can deny yourself? Explain. If not, make some space in life to work on your own growth so that your own identity can form. Find a growth group, healthy church, or other supportive context.
>
> _____
>
> _____
>
> As a couple, you may want to determine if you need to do some recovery or personal growth work in order to feel full enough to lovingly empty yourself. With whom will you do that work—or whom will you contact for references?
>
> _____
>
> _____
>
> _____

What Self-Denial Looks Like

A loving and well-thought-out attitude of self-denial will mean giving up things like these.

THE COMFORT OF DETACHMENT. Love requires the effort of making an emotional connection, even when you least feel like it. It's very natural to disconnect when you're stressed, tired, or upset with your spouse, and at times you do need "me" time. But more often, you need to deny yourself the choice of being away from relationship.

YOUR DREAMS AND DESIRES. At times, one partner

will need to postpone some good dream or legitimate desire for the sake of the connection.

THE RIGHT TO DEMAND FAIRNESS. When both partners insist on playing fair, they enter a legalistic, scorekeeping, loveless emptiness. Give more than you receive in your love life, and deny yourself the demand for fairness. Love gives up keeping score in order to gain connection and compassion.

SAYING WHATEVER YOU WANT. Learn to deny the strong urge to say to your mate exactly what you feel when you feel it. Also, just because something is true does not mean it is the most loving thing to say. Instead, when you want to say something to the person you love, ask yourself, "How would I feel if he said that to me?" This sort of approach also includes denying yourself the privilege of confronting every little thing your mate does.

THE "NOW." Love, romance, and marriage require that you often give up an immediate good for a longer-term better. Instant gratification is for children; adults practice patience, timing, and waiting. It is like the economic laws of saving and investing money: those people who can be patient and wait will always reap the greatest payoffs in the long run.

Which of these five things will you first work on giving up in order to practice "a loving and well-thought-out attitude of self-denial"?

Love is certainly free; it is a gift of God. But its full experience is costly. Comment on your experience of both aspects of this paradox of love.

A Lifeline: FREELY DENY YOURSELF THOSE THINGS THAT WOULD BE AN OBSTACLE TO THE LOVE BOTH YOU AND YOUR LOVER WANT. LOVE LIVES ARE RESCUED EVERY DAY WHEN ONE OR BOTH PARTIES SAY NO TO THE "I" FOR THE BENEFIT OF THE MUCH GREATER "WE."

Lopsided Relationships Take On Water

As you work on rescuing your love life, ask yourself these very important questions: "Is our relationship lopsided, or is it balanced? Is there a balance of choice and power? Do we tend to make decisions as a team? Does one person do more relational connecting than the other?"

What were your answers to these questions when you first read them?

_____

_____

_____

Do you think your lover would answer the questions in the same way that you did? Explain.

_____

_____

_____

The extent to which there is a balance of love and power in your relationship is the extent to which both of you will feel valued, safe, loved, and ready to move into deeper intimacy with each other. If your relationship gets too lopsided, tilting too far one way, then your love boat will take on water and eventually sink.

What Lopsidedness Looks Like

Marriages can become lopsided in relationship and in power.

LOPSIDED IN RELATIONSHIP. One person perceives inequality in the emotional investment in the relationship. The wife, for example, may feel that she is more committed and cares more. As a result, she feels unloved and not a part of his life.

If you perceive this problem in your relationship, it is always helpful to give grace to your mate first. Find out if perhaps his style of showing love and commitment is different than yours. If that effort isn't fruitful and your partner remains passive and withdrawn for some reason, confront this as a real problem. Is he afraid, disconnected, or dealing with angry feelings that he thinks, if expressed, will ruin the relationship? Get to these problems, as resolving them will help reestablish balance.

LOPSIDED IN POWER. Often, lopsidedness results when a controlling partner is matched with a more compliant one. These relationships may look OK from the outside, but all is not well. Inside the relationship, the compliant one often simply checks out and disconnects.

★ Is your relationship a match between a controlling partner and a compliant one? If so, which role do you play—and what does it feel like?

notes:

If you're the compliant one, why are you staying quiet? And what is happening to you inside while all looks good from the outside?

If you're the controlling one, have you sensed your lover's withdrawal from you? Whether or not you have, what will you do, having acknowledged that you are contributing to an unhealthy imbalance in your marriage?

Alan and Karen Right the Imbalance

Imbalance in a relationship needn't be permanent. Much connection and love can be created by couples who understand and value a "both-sided" relationship.

What aspects, if any, of Alan and Karen's relationship are similar to issues in your marriage?

"When you don't possess your half of the power equation, your passion and desire shut down. They only come out when you have self-control and freedom." What perspective on your relationship does this insight offer you?

_____

_____

_____

★ What encouragement do you find in Alan and Karen's successful resolution of their balance of power issue?

_____

_____

_____

Alan and Karen successfully moved from a one-sided relationship to a relationship characterized by healthy mutuality.

Where's the Power?

When you talk with your partner about the power balance in your relationship, you will probably conclude that it's not exactly 50/50. Few relationships are. In most, one person tends to take more initiative, and the other is more responsive. This doesn't necessarily indicate a one-sided relationship.

Describing your relationship in terms of initiative and responsiveness rather than control and compliance may be more accurate. Is your relationship a match between a partner who naturally tends to take more initiative and one who is more responsive? If so, which role do you play—and what does it feel like?

_____

_____

_____

If this is your situation, it doesn't necessarily mean you have a major problem. But you both need to look at the pattern. The less assertive person should ask herself and her partner, "If I did want to speak up more, do I feel the freedom and support from you to do that?" The more assertive person needs to be sure to always look for, ask for, and be truly open to the feelings and opinions of his partner.

In some couples, one partner may truly be dominating and not allowing mutuality, and consequently his lover feels controlled, unloved, and dismissed. Are you playing one of these two roles? Are you living by the motto "peace at any price"? If so, are you experiencing real peace, which brings warmth and vulnerability, or more of a truce?

From the outside, an imbalanced relationship may seem calm and without conflict, but often underneath is a sense of alienation, disconnection, hurt, and even anger.

Moving Back to Mutuality

Whether you have a slightly or seriously lopsided relationship, you can take some steps to rescue your relationship from taking on water. Here are some ideas.

SLAVES GO FIRST. The partner who feels controlled—the "slave"—is generally the one who needs to make the first step. So if you're the slave, break out of your shackles!

Tell your lover you want to feel all the love, passion, desire, and longing for him that is in you. You want to give him everything you have. A mate would have to be pretty dumb to argue against that! Tell him that, in order for you to experience those feelings, you must have more of the power and decision-making in the relationship's choices and directions. In your own words, how will you communicate this to him?

_____

_____

ADMIT YOUR PART OF THE PROBLEM. Often, the "slave" has brought this issue of passivity and compliance into the relationship.

Admit your contribution: your fear of conflict, your fear of responsibility for decisions, or your fear of failure. That will help your partner to know he is not being seen as the ogre. If you have more control in the relationship, acknowledge your part in the problem and give up some territory. Have you simply not been paying attention to the dynamics of your relationship? Do you struggle to allow your partner to have choices because you'll feel helpless and out of control? Is the issue more a matter of self-centeredness? Of entitlement? Something else?

_____

_____

_____

COME BACK TO RELATIONSHIP. Keep the main things the main things: relationship, closeness, and love. Don't get sidetracked into focusing simply on choice and decision. Appeal to what you both want most: the connection. And that connection can be rescued and strengthened.

★What is your understanding of this statement: "choice and decision must serve your need to give and receive love"?

_____

_____

_____

What, if anything, do you need to do to make these words your own? "I want us both to be in charge of this relationship. This isn't simply about me wanting more choices, though I do. This is more about how sharing decisions will help me feel closer to you and more a part of 'us.'"

_____

_____

_____

SET LIMITS. If the control problem does not resolve itself—if your mate continues to be too controlling—the relationship may require you to set some limits and establish some boundaries. The resulting consequences can help you maintain your stance that you insist on being able to make choices in the relationship.

When have you experienced the consequences of ignoring someone's boundaries? What, if anything, did you learn from those consequences?

_____

_____

Give an example of a boundary you could establish for your controlling mate. What, for instance, would be a viable consequence the next time he makes a decision without consulting you? The next time she fills your weekend calendar without talking to you about the activities?

Good relationships and struggling relationships all benefit when defined by clear delineations of power, choice, and respect for each other.

You both need choices. You both need power. You both need self-control. And when your connection protects and supports the balanced, two-sided relationship, love has room and encouragement to grow. And passion, desire, and intimacy are often the fruits of mutuality.

A Lifeline: GIVE UP SOME TERRITORY FOR THE GREAT-EST GIFT GOD PROVIDES: A TRULY SATISFYING RELATIONSHIP. IN VIEW OF THE RETURNS, IT IS NO REAL SACRIFICE.

Living What I Learn

Which of this session's five topics did you find most relevant or helpful? Explain.

❏ The Real Scoop About Happiness
❏ Are They Needs or Desires?
❏ Stop Looking for Your Other Half
❏ Self-Denial? You're Joking, Right?
❏ Lopsided Relationships Take On Water

_____

_____

_____

★ Share one or two insights from the text that you found especially encouraging.

_____

_____

Which of the following lifelines will you grab this week? What specific step(s) will you take to help rescue yourself and thereby rescue your marriage?

❑ Take ownership of your own happiness.

❑ You can keep your love life on course by not disconnecting when your preferences are not met and by always working to meet each other's real needs.

❑ To preserve the connection between you and your spouse, remember that you both are still cooking. Be sure the right ingredients are in the mix—love, honesty, support, feedback, and becoming whole yourself. And give your mate time to learn and grow.

❑ Freely deny yourself of the things that would be an obstacle to the love both you and your lover both want. Say no to the "I" for benefit of the much greater "we."

❑ Give up some territory for the greatest gift God provides: a truly satisfying relationship. In view of the returns, it is no real sacrifice.

_____

_____

If you have asked someone to hold you accountable in your efforts to rescue your marriage, what effect, if any, did that accountability have on your rescue efforts this week? If you haven't yet asked someone to hold you accountable, what step did you take this week to find someone—or what step will you take in the next seven days?

_____

As you close in prayer, ask God to help you be open to His transforming touch so that He can make your expectations reasonable and appropriate—and make you open to wanting to meet your mate's reasonable and appropriate expectations of you.

When you go to the meeting, be ready to . . .
- Share your answers to the starred (★) questions.
- Choose which of the lifelines you'll grab and work on this week.

During the week . . .
- As you work on your section 2 lifeline, pay attention to the effects of your efforts on you, on your mate, and on your marriage.

DUMB ATTITUDE #3

"My Lover Should Be Perfect for Me"

Y ou're learning to look at your own issues and live in reality with your spouse. Now you're ready to deal with the fact that you are to help each other grow.

Couples who help each other accept and then grow beyond their own needs and imperfections are well on the way to rescuing their relationship. Which of your needs and imperfections make you worry that your mate won't accept you?

_____

_____

_____

Which of your mate's needs and imperfections make it difficult for you to wholeheartedly accept him? Ask for the Lord's help!

_____

_____

Both of you have needs and weaknesses. They may be big or little, but they are *real*. They exist. And when it comes to love, you are always on better footing when you deal with what is rather than what should be.

In what ways, if any, are you not dealing with "what is" about yourself? About your marriage? Why?

_____

_____

_____

What, if anything, is keeping you from letting your partner know you on a real-life level?

_____

_____

_____

When you connect with your lover's frailties in order to help him overcome them, you are giving grace at a deep level. And that grace always brings forth good things in a connection. It is also beneficial in the other direction: when your spouse helps you in your own weakness, you then experience love, acceptance, safety, and gratitude.

When have you experienced such grace—and the love, acceptance, safety, and gratitude that go with it—from your spouse or someone else? What impact did it have on you?

_____

_____

_____

> What impact might your extension of grace—and love, acceptance, safety and gratitude—have on your spouse?
>
> _____
>
> _____
>
> _____

Don't run from your partner's needs and weaknesses. They won't go away anyway. Instead, be a redemptive, healing force for your mate, and you will bring love and intimacy to your connection.

> *Lord God, facing needs and accepting weaknesses—that's not necessarily an easy or comfortable assignment. Please give me the grace and courage I need to face my own flaws and to accept my weaknesses as well as abundant grace to extend to my spouse. Help me embrace my spouse despite the flaws and weaknesses that, frankly, I have an easier time seeing than my own. Please also give me the desire and ability to nurture my spouse's needs, to express my own needs, and to, by Your grace and transforming power, become a better lover. In Jesus's name. Amen.*

There Are No Perfect 10s

Ryan pulled out an actual list of traits he wanted in the woman he married—and girlfriend Jen just didn't match up! No one could have!

Be honest—and not too hard on Ryan. Do you have a list of traits (in your mind, if not on a piece of paper) that you want in your spouse? Could anyone meet all those criteria?

_____

_____

_____

Do you, like Ryan, find yourself thinking (too much) about "all the things [your spouse] isn't"? What does your answer to that question mean to you?

_____

_____

_____

The Problem of the Ideal

One of the biggest relationship killers around is *comparing the person you love to a fantasy*. The truth is, the real person can never match up to the fantasy. The comparison to the fantasy has to die in order for love to live.

When, if ever, have you been compared to a fantasy and, of course, not measured up? Comment on what that felt like.

_____

_____

_____

To what fantasy, or to what specific aspect of another person, are you comparing your lover?

_____

_____

_____

As Ryan realized, *either the ideal dies or love dies.* The fantasy of finding someone perfect to make you happy is just that—a fantasy. Real love can only exist with a less-than-perfect person, as the world contains no other kind.

★ What freedom comes with seeing the truth that the world only contains less-than-perfect people?

_____

_____

_____

Any quality you admire in the person you are fantasizing about is not being seen in the context of a real relationship, with real problems involving all that person's inevitable imperfections, conflicts, selfishness, and the like. As you let that truth sink in, consider which, if any, of the following situations from real relationships you can identify with— and what that reveals to you about yourself.

❑ You look at your spouse's body and see more of what is wrong than what you like. The result is that you feel indifferent or turned off.

❑ You notice some talent or trait of another person, compare that to your spouse, and get a sinking feeling.

❑ Your spouse interacts with you in some way, and you go away wishing that you were married to someone who is not like that.

❑ You have a "partial" relationship with someone, such as a co-worker, that does not involve interacting with the whole person in a real relationship, and you fantasize that being with that person would be better than being with your mate.

❑ You look at fantasy material in magazines, the Internet, or the movies and wish you had someone like that. Or you read romance novels or watch romantic movies and wish your husband were like the hero in the story.

❑ You look back at a teenage love or the one that got away and longingly compare your mate to that person.

❑ You look at who your spouse is not, or who she is in comparison to your expectations, more than who she is in terms of the things you love about her.

Real love is found with real people, all of whom possess both beauty and flaws, good qualities and imperfections. If you chase a fantasy, you are going to hate reality. But reality is the only place you can find real and satisfying love.

Who, if anyone, has loved you even though he was fully aware of your beauty *and* your flaws, your good qualities *and* your imperfections?

_____

★ What can you do to kill the fantasy? Be specific.

_____

_____

_____

What, if anything in addition to unrealistic expectations, is keeping you from offering your lover that kind of love?

_____

_____

Don't allow a fantasy to interrupt building real love with a real person. Certainly, you could always look at your lover and see how someone else would be better in some way. But you are not in a real relationship with someone else. You are just in a fantasy with a specific part of that other person, such as physical beauty or an isolated personality component. So throw away your list of ideals. It is getting in the way of loving the real person you are with.

This Is Not Disneyland, So Grow Up!

Part of the adult vow we take when we marry is "for better or for worse." Perhaps the vow ought to say "for better *and* for worse," because the truth is, there's no "or" involved; the better *and* the worse will certainly come in marriage.

What "worse" has your lover seen in you since the two of you said, "I do"?

The "worse" in your lover may come to mind all too easily. So take a few minutes right now to make an actual list (yes, with pen or pencil on paper) of the "better," of the good you've seen in your lover. That's a solid initial step toward conditioning yourself to focus on the good that really is there.

A Lifeline: BECOME THE HERO AND RESCUE YOUR RELATIONSHIP FROM FANTASYLAND AND THE RESIDENT VILE KILLER—COMPARISON TO THE IDEAL PERSON WHO DOESN'T EXIST IN REALITY AND WHOM YOUR MATE IS NOT AND NEVER WILL BE. STOP THE COMPARISONS, LOVE THE ONE YOU ARE WITH, AND YOUR DREAM CAN COME TRUE. YOU CAN LIVE HAPPILY, THOUGH IMPERFECTLY, EVER AFTER.

notes:

Pour On the Grace

Consider this dilemma:

1. You and your lover both need copious amounts of grace and love.
2. It's your responsibility to give large amounts of grace and love to each other.
3. You probably don't have enough grace and love to give.

Give evidence from your relationship that you and your lover face this dilemma—and realize that every couple faces this same dilemma.

_____

_____

_____

The reality is that, to solve this problem, we have to go outside the relationship to replenish our supply of grace. What's your initial reaction to this truth? Are you already acting on this truth? If so, why—and if not, why not?

_____

_____

_____

Couples who go outside the relationship to replenish their supply of grace find their connection with each other strengthened and steadied.

Remember Megan and Will's situation (Book pg. 75)? What did you appreciate about the way Will dealt with his sin?

What did you most admire about Megan's course of action?

What does Megan and Will's experience illustrate about both the importance and the power of grace in rescuing a love life? Address Megan's attitude as well as Will's involvement in a group.

You Need More Than You Think

Grace is undeserved favor. We want to help you focus on how the need for grace is experienced and understood, so that you can learn to provide it for your lover.

Most of us don't realize the enormous amount of grace we need in our marriage relationship. Every couple needs a big helping of grace to go deeper, reconnect, take risks, forgive, accept, be truthful, and help each other reach intimacy.

★ Share your own thoughts as to why grace is key to an intimate marriage.

Not only is our need for grace great, but most of us have negative and critical voices in our heads that fight off grace: "I shouldn't be that way"; "I should be stronger"; "I'm a loser"; "I don't deserve to be treated well after what I've done." What voice in your head needs to be defeated by grace so that you can allow your mate inside?

_____

_____

_____

In order to respond to, if not completely silence, those voices, get feedback from balanced people who are *for* you when you hear these voices. Their grace and truth can help modify and mature those voices into more realistic and loving words.

_____

_____

_____

Couples who are aware of their deep need for undeserved favor are starting at the right place. *The need that both of you have for undeserved favor can draw you together emotionally, personally, and spiritually.*

Do you have an easy time asking others to meet your need? Why or why not?

_____

_____

Where there is no need, there can be no needs met. The relationship becomes a nonevent. What need will you acknowledge to yourself and then share with your mate? Doing so will help your relationship.

_____

Don't make the mistake of thinking you only need to give grace to each other during bad times and struggles. Divinely bestowed grace is not just for broken things like problems, hurts, and failure. It is also meant for the sustenance and maintenance of life and love. Grace should be the norm of a relationship, not the exception.

When has the presence of friction, disconnection, or misunderstanding clued you in to the fact that one or both of you are in need of grace?

_____

_____

_____

The best place to begin rescuing your love life is for both of you to come to the end of yourselves and admit to each other that you need each other's grace—not today, not once, but every day and in every way. When, if ever, have you admitted to your lover your need for her grace? What did that bold and vulnerable statement do for your relationship? If you haven't ever been this open with your spouse, when will you?

_____

_____

_____

When has your lover ever admitted the need for grace from you? If that has happened, what are you doing to provide that grace "every day and in every way"? If your lover has not yet admitted the need for grace, what do you want your response to be like when the admission comes?

_____

_____

_____

The Task and Responsibility to Give Grace

Take on the task of being alert to your lover's need for grace. Though ultimately each partner is responsible for getting her needs met, the best couples are always concerned about meeting the needs of the other.

BE GRACIOUS IN YOUR CONTENT AND TONE. We administer grace to each other by both the content and the tone of what we say.

Content has to do with letting your spouse know in words that you care, the extent of how much you care, and what you value about him (see the list on Book pg. 78). It's important to tell your lover how you feel about her. Don't assume she always knows. You refuel your car regularly, because gas burns up. The same is true with grace. What message of grace will you offer your lover today?

_____

_____

_____

Tone is the way you speak, and your tone should be caring and warm, drawing your lover in, not distancing her. You may find it helpful to put yourself in your spouse's place and listen to yourself. How would you feel if you were on the receiving end of the grace you're extending? Consider the content as well as tone. Would you feel dismissed, cold, misunderstood? Or would you feel cherished and loved, understood and accepted? What changes in your content as well as in your tone or delivery might you make so that your lover feels loved and accepted?

_____

_____

_____

_____

BE A STUDENT OF YOUR LOVER. Grace is a universal need, but it is often administered in a highly individual and personal way. Observe your lover and get to know her so that you can give her the grace she needs.

Remember the list of things to watch for in your lover? Make some notes here:

· What is she insecure about?

_____

· What makes her happy?

_____

· What scares her?

_____

· What does she feel is wrong with her?

_____

· What does she need to hear often?

_____

· What does she dream of?

_____

· What does she want from the relationship?

_____

What will you do and/or say to affirm and support your lover in these areas?

_____

_____

_____

_____

_____

Undeserved Means Undeserved

Grace—in the Christian faith, in a marriage, anywhere—cannot be earned or merited (Ephesians 2:8–9). You and your partner qualify for each other's grace on a need basis, not on a performance basis.

Our natural tendency is to give love when our spouse acts lovingly toward us and to withhold love when he disconnects from us. When has someone given you grace when you definitely didn't earn it or deserve it? What were your feelings toward that person? Would those feelings help build intimacy in your marriage? Explain.

_____

_____

_____

You may wonder exactly what to say when you want to offer your lover grace. Here are a couple of ideas. When he is being selfish, say, "What you are doing feels selfish to me, and it distances me. But I want to deal with this because I want us to be OK." If she has been hurtful or critical, you might say, "What you said really bothers me. Part of me wants to walk away right now. But I know we need to talk about this and get it straight. I don't want it to come between us." Practice saying these—or similar—statements out loud so you can do it in real time when you need to.

_____

_____

_____

Give your lover grace by taking the first step to move toward her. Be for her, be for the relationship, and face the issue so that you can resolve it and move on with each other. You may need to grow thicker skin in order to give her the favors that she and your connection need.

This is not about creating positive feelings in a struggling relationship. Feelings don't come because we want them to. The path that works is to be *for* you and her and the relationship, to connect as much as you can, and to be in the process of growth. These steps will create the feelings you want.

★ Be specific. What will "being for your spouse" look like and sound like?

★ What will "being for the relationship" look like and sound like?

What are some surefire or almost-surefire ways to connect with your mate?

In what ways are you "in the process of growth"? Put differently, what are you doing to grow as a spouse who can—and will—extend grace to your lover sincerely and constantly?

Don't try to make yourself feel things; you can't do it. Create a context of grace that will grow the feelings.

Get Grace from the Outside

As we have said, you don't possess all the grace you need for yourself and for your partner. You both need more grace than there is in the relationship. A couple who exists in a bubble, without others supporting them, is a couple who will be in trouble at some level.

What kind of support for your marriage do you and your spouse receive? If you don't receive support, what keeps you from seeking it out?

_____

_____

_____

At times, through no one's fault, you won't have enough grace for each other. You may be drained from work, fatigue, or stress; you'll feel alienated or disconnected from your lover. This is normal and expected; it is part of love. When, if ever, has anyone told you that before? Why is that good news?

_____

_____

_____

During these periods of disconnect, don't pull away and don't pretend to feel things you don't feel. These approaches don't work, so instead choose the path of humility. What might the path of humility look like?

_____

_____

_____

Humility means admitting your need and getting more grace from outside your marriage. What outside sources will you look to for the grace you need?

_____

_____

_____

The key source of grace we can extend to our lover is our relationship with God. What do you do in the course of a normal day—and a normal week—to strengthen your relationship with God, the Author of love and grace?

_____

_____

_____

★Admitting our need and filling our emptiness from good sources is a far cry from our natural tendency to "try harder," "suck it up," and "commit more." It's much better to receive, experience, and lavish grace. What can you do to counter that natural tendency? Finding an accountability partner, for instance, may help.

_____

_____

_____

The most connected couples you'll meet are not just connected to each other, but also to others who are caring, safe, full of grace, and supportive of their relationship with their partner. You don't weaken your marriage by having other relationships; you infuse it with the favor you want to lavish on each other.

A Lifeline: STOP AND EXPERIENCE YOUR NEED FOR GRACE. GRACE CANNOT BE ADMINISTERED UNTIL THE NEED IS ADMITTED. ALSO, MAKE IT A HABIT TO BE GENEROUS WITH GRACE. YOU CAN NEVER OVERGRACE YOUR RELATIONSHIP.

Sometimes Your Lover Needs a Nudge

Couples who do well in closeness, attachment, and love have experience with something I (John) call *the nudge*—a healthy and balanced confrontation intended to push each other to be more than they are. Nudges tend to produce really good relational results.

Think about how Ross's wife, Anne, nudged him to follow his dream and start his own business. The nudging resonated with Ross, and he set out on his own. It was a little scary for a couple of years, but then his business became successful. The competency that Anne saw in him paid off, and now they are doing very well. What nudge do you think your lover needs from you right now?

_____

_____

★ The person who knows you best should be able to see not only who you are, but who you can be. Spend some time brainstorming on who you see your spouse becoming. Think about all aspects of life: spiritual, emotional, mental, and professional. What can you do—with gentle nudges, not nagging—to encourage this growth?

_____

When you make nudging acceptable in a relationship, and when nudging works, you both get the reconnections and intimacy you want and need.

Expectations Are OK

Nudges have to do with seeing that each of you can be more than you are and helping each other on that path. They have to do with our *expectations* of each other. *You are to love each other enough to expect your partner to grow into more than he is right now.*

What healthy and loving expectations do you have for your spouse? Jot a few specifics down here. Do you, for instance, want your mate to be more loving, responsible, spiritual, real, or honest?

Having higher expectations does not mean that you don't accept your mate as he is today. No one grows or truly changes from the heart unless he is first accepted as he is. Does your mate know that you truly accept him? On what do you base your answer? If you're not sure, ask—and find out what you could do to underscore your total acceptance and love of your spouse. There is really no conflict between acceptance and expectations. In fact, they are partners in intimacy.

Having standards, requirements, or expectations for your spouse is not the same as being critical or unaccepting. But do pause and consider the way you express your standards and expectations. What do your delivery and your tone communicate?

_____

_____

_____

What is your response—or what would you like it to be—when your lover shares expectations of you?

_____

_____

_____

★ Do you really believe this statement: "If I didn't want you to be more than you are, I would not really be loving you"? Explain your answer.

_____

_____

_____

Expectations, challenges, and rules are good for you and good for your love. When you have reasonable and good standards, you are defining what you want and need. You are establishing a healthy structure for love to grow. You are letting your partner know what will help you two be together and happy.

Why You Need Expectations

John Lennon and Paul McCartney wrote many great songs, but they were wrong about "all you need is love." You do need love, and lots of it, but you also need to be honest, to confront, and to have expectations of each other. None of us grows and blossoms without both. Why is this? Here are some reasons.

EXPECTATIONS GET YOU OUT OF THE COMFORT ZONE. When two people become committed to each other or married, they almost always start regressing into comfortable and nongrowing patterns.

What comfortable, nongrowing pattern, if any, did you and your partner slip into? Think about working out, personal grooming, and giving each other undivided attention.

_____

_____

This regressive force can create a real problem if the "me" you regress into tends to be unloving, self-involved, disengaged, lazy, controlling, or irresponsible. That's the comfort zone. Have you fallen into it? If so, why are you still there?

_____

_____

The comfort zone is also where fears live. When we are afraid of failure, conflict, or change, we stay in a state of paralysis and become comfortable with that. If you're in the comfort zone, is fear rather than laziness the main reason? What would be a healthy way of dealing with that fear?

_____

_____

If your lover is in the comfort zone, is fear rather than laziness the main reason? What might you do to help your lover out of this zone?

_____

_____

_____

Whether the comfort zone is from regression or fear, lovers should give each other permission to nudge each other out of it. When expectations and requirements are given lovingly and not harshly, they can be welcome and effective.

EXPECTATIONS HELP YOU SEE YOUR BLIND SPOTS. We are often unaware of when we aren't being our best. Who better than your mate to point out something you are doing that is hindering your own growth, development, and success?

What if your partner said, "I want you to push more, take some risks, and stop being satisfied with the average"? Would you be hurt? Confused? Or would you be energized with new vision? Why do you think you would react that way?

_____

_____

_____

Does your mate have a long-held dream to pursue or a talent that she is not aware of? You have a duty to see it, know it, and let your lover know that you want her to follow the dream or develop that talent.

_____

_____

_____

We can be blind to problems as well as to dreams and talents. Specifically, we are often unaware of things we do to hurt each other and ourselves. What do you want your response to be when your partner approaches you about a problem in your blind spot?

_____

_____

_____

What do you want your approach to be when you need to approach your partner about a problem in a blind spot?

_____

_____

_____

_____

When it's your turn to speak, choose words that are not critical, mean, or judgmental. And when it's your turn to listen, accept your spouse's words as an attempt to deal with a blind spot and rescue the love life. It is an act of love, not of control.

EXPECTATIONS HELP YOU AND YOUR PARTNER GROW TOGETHER. When you grow as individuals, you grow as lovers. Partners who encourage each other to be all that they can be and see positive results in each other tend to be closer, more romantic, and more interested in each other.

When have you seen this truth in real life?

_____

_____

_____

When, if ever, have you experienced the truth that love and people grow together?

_____

_____

We hope you're not settling into "That's just how I am." What are you doing—or could you be doing—to grow? If you are becoming a better and more developed person personally, emotionally, and spiritually, your heart is being enlarged, and that translates to a direct benefit for the connection.

_____

_____

_____

Where to Start

Here are some things you can do to "nudge" your love life along.

WALK OUT OF THE COMFORT ZONE. Talk about how the two of you want to be safe, accepting, and unconditional in your love. But at the same time, humbly submit to each other in growth areas and problems.

What would walking out of the comfort zone look like in your relationship?

_____

_____

_____

More specifically, what undeveloped things in yourself might your lover want to help develop?

_____

_____

_____

What undeveloped things in your lover do you want to help develop?

What problems that disconnect you do you want to help solve?

BECOME A TEAM. Work together on what each of you wants for yourself and your mate. Be a partner, an encourager, and a coach. Make it something for the two of you.

Think about something you two could work on together. What can you do to model, for instance, being a better listener?

★ What will you do to be sure you're a coachable partner when your lover approaches you about something?

CELEBRATE CHANGE. When one of you makes a few moves in the right direction, celebrate it! When your lover makes the effort and takes the risk, even a small one, affirm and reinforce him.

When has affirmation encouraged you to keep on keeping on?

_____

_____

_____

What, if anything, might keep you from giving that same gift to your lover? Do what you can to remove those roadblocks.

_____

_____

_____

The best gift for change is yourself. Give him your love, your admiration, your respect, and your attention. Let him know that his steps to be all that he can be will bring him even more of you than he has now.

A Lifeline: LIFE IS NOT MEANT TO BE ABOUT SETTLING FOR THE STATUS QUO. IT IS A TEMPLATE FOR US TO BECOME SOMETHING MUCH BETTER THAN WE ARE, AND RELATIONSHIPS CAN PROVIDE THE GROUNDWORK FOR THAT TO HAPPEN.

Vive les Différences

Differences should not be a problem in your relationship. In fact, the opposite is true. Differences are a necessary component for finding, keeping, and sharing the love life we all want. When one partner resists the other's differences, she risks losing the love she would like to develop.

When you think about differences between you and your lover, what character qualities and personal tastes come to mind? Name three or four.

_____

_____

_____

★ This may be a new perspective for you, but in what way do the differences you just listed enhance your relationship?

_____

_____

_____

Differences Help Create Love

How can differences help two people rescue their love lives? The answer lies in the contrast between immature and mature love.

Immature love seeks sameness and similarity. When you first met your lover, what similar interests, likes, dislikes, and preferences served as glue for the early stages of your relationship?

_____

_____

Love begins with alliance and similarity, but as the relationship develops, differences begin to emerge, as they should. In what ways have your life and perspective been enhanced and stretched by your partner's varying views and experiences? Give one or two examples.

_____

_____

_____

Love seeks out growth. It isn't threatened by differences; it enjoys them. Because of his differences, you see that other person as interesting, sometimes challenging, and able to show you new ways of relating to life.

Couples are different in a lot of ways. Which of the following differences (described on Book pgs. 88–89) do you find in your relationship—and who's who?

❏ *Feelers and thinkers*

❏ *Extroverts and introverts*

❏ *Active types and reflective types*

★ Nurturing each other includes encouraging, appreciating, and connecting with each other's differences. What can you do to appreciate your lover's differences? To connect with them?

When you support the individual styles and preferences of your lover, he truly feels that you know him for who he really is. This is the opposite of feeling criticized, put down, or shamed for simply being yourself.

Don't Moralize Your Differences

Beware of the tendency to make your own opinion a moral issue rather than an apples-versus-oranges preference. There is no one "right way" between feelers and thinkers, extroverts and introverts, or active and reflective types.

Different isn't always an issue of right versus wrong. What differences between you and your lover have you thought about in terms of right and wrong? What freedom will come with just accepting them as different?

_____

_____

_____

★ Matters of style and preference don't fall into the categories of right and wrong. What can you do to be more accommodating of your lover's differences? Stay open, appreciative, and even protective of your partner's individuality.

_____

_____

_____

Get Rid of Destructive Differences

Certain types of differences that are not just matters of style or preference are actually problems, and they cause negative things to happen in relationships. These destructive differences come out of a person's brokenness, baggage from the past, immaturities, or character issues. (Remember Stan and Michele's sad situation?)

Pay attention to these hurtful sorts of differences, for they can do a lot of damage to the love you are trying to create. Which, if any, of the following truly destructive differences do you find in your marriage?

Irresponsibility   Control

Criticism and judgment   Manipulation

Self-centeredness   Rage

Guilt messages   Deception

Addictions   Violence

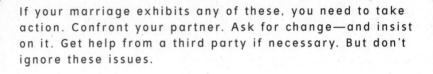

If your marriage exhibits any of these, you need to take action. Confront your partner. Ask for change—and insist on it. Get help from a third party if necessary. But don't ignore these issues.

If you're not sure whether differences between you and your lover are style differences or destructive differences, look at them through the following three-part lens.

THEY CUT OFF LOVE AND TRUST. Destructive differences destroy intimacy and sink your love life. You cannot trust, be safe with, or be totally vulnerable with someone who is not honest, dependable, or in control of himself.

THEY REDUCE FREEDOM. Destructive differences don't leave the other partner feeling free to make choices and speak the truth.

THEY ARE ABOUT "ME," NOT "US." The other partner finds himself worrying about, protecting himself from, or trying to fix the differences. This is a far cry from the fun of observing and interacting with your lover's quirks and individuality.

Do these three traits characterize the differences between you and your partner? If not, don't worry about them. Instead, as was just stated, enjoy your lover's quirks and individuality.

If your partner's differences cut off love and trust, reduce freedom, or are about him, stand up to these destructive differences. Confront your partner. Tell him you won't tolerate how they affect the relationship. Work with him to find help (small groups, churches, therapy).

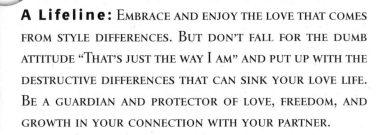

A Lifeline: EMBRACE AND ENJOY THE LOVE THAT COMES FROM STYLE DIFFERENCES. BUT DON'T FALL FOR THE DUMB ATTITUDE "THAT'S JUST THE WAY I AM" AND PUT UP WITH THE DESTRUCTIVE DIFFERENCES THAT CAN SINK YOUR LOVE LIFE. BE A GUARDIAN AND PROTECTOR OF LOVE, FREEDOM, AND GROWTH IN YOUR CONNECTION WITH YOUR PARTNER.

Getting to the Heart of Feelings

One of the most powerful keys to an intimate and passionate love life is also one of the most unnatural and counterintuitive things you will ever do. It is called *validation*, and it refers to your ability to understand and empathize with the feelings and experiences of your lover, *especially when your view is not his.*

What is your initial reaction to this assignment? Does it seem like "Mission: Impossible"? Why or why not?

notes:

★ Based on the definition of *validation* that you just read, explain why it is key to a fulfilling love life.

_____

_____

Notice that validation is especially important when your mate's view and your view don't match—and, even more especially, when he sees something negative in your own behavior that you do not see in that way. What do you want your response to your mate to be in that situation?

_____

_____

★ Validation has to do with drawing him out and helping him feel that you truly hear him on a deep level. It's making him know that you really understand his feelings. What might be some ways to do that? Be specific.

_____

_____

_____

Proverbs 20:5 says, "The purposes of a man's heart are deep waters, but a man of understanding draws them out." As you help your mate express his heart and be understood, you are drawing him out.

Why Validation?

Validation is necessary for couples to navigate successfully through conflict because we all have a need to be heard and understood. We really don't move forward to resolve conflicts when we do not feel we have been understood.

Think about the last fight you had with your partner. When you were trying to get your feelings across, did your partner minimize, dismiss, or simply not understand what you were saying? What was that like for you?

In what ways did your partner's response to the feelings you shared affect your ability and desire to hear his side of things?

Most likely, not receiving validation from your mate disconnected things even further. Such a lack of validation essentially puts your heart in prison: you have expressed your views, but you feel that you have not been heard. You are left all by yourself with your viewpoint, feelings, and experiences. Yet you are required to hear your partner's side—the bad things you have done. This imprisonment generally results in disconnection, guilt, false external compliance, anger, and a host of other reactions that will tear a relationship apart.

Is your partner receiving validation from you? Give evidence from a recent fight to support your answer.

Why are you sure that your validation of your partner is being received by him as such?

In what ways/with what actions are you putting your spouse in a prison of, among other things, disconnection, guilt, false external compliance, and anger? If you don't know, ask!

When couples learn to validate each other's experiences, they feel that their partner is part of their life again. They no longer feel alone.

Remember the backyard barbecue when the wife joins in on a joke about the husband's thinning hair? That evening, the husband says to his wife, "I can't believe you. In front of the neighborhood, you put me down about my hair. Thanks so much for the embarrassment." What is one response that would address the situation and, perhaps more importantly, validate your lover?

Validation would sound something like, "I'm really sorry, honey. That must have been awkward, especially in front of our friends." What is another way you could say this? As you write down one or two practice statements, be sure to keep the essential element present. Let your mate know that you are attempting to understand what the experience was like from his perspective.

Be sure you understand this: *validation has nothing to do with whether you agree or disagree with your partner.* Validating your mate's feelings as being important and real to him does not mean you accept his view as truth and reality.

Validation comes first, and then comes reality. People are much more open to hearing facts after their viewpoint has been validated. Is that true for you? Give an example from your own life.

What will you do—or what do you already do—to validate your spouse's point of view? When things start to get hot, validate. That should help the other person to calm down and be more receptive. Then close the conversation with, "Are we OK on this?"

Sometimes validation can help pave the way to resolving the problem and resuming the connection. And sometimes validation is the resolution itself. Simply being heard is often enough. When has "simply being heard" been enough for you?

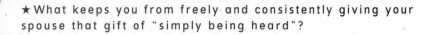

★ What keeps you from freely and consistently giving your spouse that gift of "simply being heard"?

_____

_____

_____

When I (John) complained to Barbi about what a rotten weekend it was turning out to be, she just listened and said, "Yes, I guess it really is a pretty crummy weekend for you, not being able to relax and enjoy anything." I felt better, because she got it. Nothing about the circumstances of the weekend changed. Barbi and I still had to play out the weekend schedule. But we were connected, because we were together in the weekend.

The Work of Validation

Validation is unnatural; it takes work. Here we will list for you the kind of work that will help you and your partner validate each other.

GET OUT OF THE WAY. Learn to suspend your own point of view, to put your way of seeing things aside in order to leave room for your partner's feelings and experiences, and to give up the attempt to be seen as good, innocent, or right.

GO FIRST TO EMPATHY. When you know your partner is upset, angry, or hurt, think first about figuring out and understanding how he is feeling and why. This is an act of grace and love: "Do to others as you would have them do to you" (Luke 6:31).

ASK; DON'T ANSWER. Get to the pain and emotions. Don't try to answer the problem or fix it. Open things; don't close them. Instead of saying, "Well, you'll feel better later," say, "That sounds awful; tell me more."

CHECK IT OUT. When your lover explains her viewpoint, ask if you are understanding her experience. Even if you are off base, she is likely to appreciate your effort to connect with her experience and perspective.

LIVE WITH THE TENSION OF UNHAPPINESS. Feelings take time to resolve, and they cannot be rushed. So be patient, present, and empathic. Your mate's unhappy feelings won't last. Stay for the long haul.

Which of these five kinds of work are you already doing?

_____

_____

_____

Which work of validation is especially challenging for you?

_____

_____

_____

What will you do to overcome that challenge and validate your lover in that particular way?

_____

_____

_____

_____

Validation reaches into the heart of your lover so that the two of you can reconnect and deal with the problem between you. When you reach the point where you both feel you have been heard and understood by each other, then you are ready to grapple with the problem.

What issue do you and your lover need to resolve? Did one of you do a hurtful thing and need to apologize, take responsibility, and change? Or did one of you make a mistake, or are the two of you suffering the consequences of miscommunication?

_____

_____

Are you at the point where you both feel you've been heard and understood by each other? Support your answer with evidence.

_____

_____

_____

 A Lifeline: WHATEVER THE NATURE OF THE CONFLICT, USE VALIDATION TO MAKE YOURSELVES ALLIES, NOT ADVERSARIES, AS YOU DEAL WITH WHAT YOU NEED TO DEAL WITH.

Living What I Learn

Which of this section's five topics did you find most relevant or helpful? Explain.

❑ There Are No Perfect 10s
❑ Pour On the Grace
❑ Sometimes Your Lover Needs a Nudge
❑ _Vive les Différences_
❑ Getting to the Heart of Feelings

_____

_____

★ Share one or two insights from the text that you found especially encouraging.

_____

_____

_____

Which of the following lifelines will you grab this week? What specific step(s) will you take to help rescue yourself and thereby rescue your marriage?

❏ Rescue your love life from fantasyland and the resident vile killer—comparison and demands to be ideal.

❏ Stop and experience your need for grace. Grace cannot be administered until the need is admitted. Also, make it a habit to be generous with grace. You can never overgrace your relationship.

❏ Life is not meant to be all that comfortable. It is a template for each of us to become something much better than we are, and relationships can provide the groundwork for that to happen.

❏ Embrace and enjoy the love that comes from style differences. Be a guardian and protector of love, freedom, and growth in your connection with your partner.

❏ Whatever the nature of the conflict, use validation to make yourselves allies, not adversaries, as you deal with what you need to deal with.

_____

_____

_____

As you close in prayer, ask the Lord to help you do just that by the power of His grace and with His love.

When you go to the meeting, be ready to . . .

• SHARE YOUR ANSWERS TO THE STARRED (★) QUESTIONS.

• CHOOSE WHICH OF THE LIFELINES YOU'LL GRAB AND WORK ON THIS WEEK.

During the week . . .

• AS YOU WORK ON YOUR SECTION 3 LIFELINE, PAY ATTENTION TO THE EFFECTS OF YOUR EFFORTS ON YOU, ON YOUR MATE, AND ON YOUR MARRIAGE.

DUMB ATTITUDE #4

"My Lover Should Never Hurt Me"

Think about the last time you looked at your mate and thought, *I really don't like this person very much right now.* This is a pretty normal experience at some point for most couples.

What did you think when you first realized that you wouldn't always like the person you promised to always love?

_____

_____

_____

What is helpful about realizing that all of us are imperfect people, and we all love imperfectly?

_____

_____

_____

There is a lot you can do to rescue your love life from the dumb attitude that says, "My lover should never hurt me!" In this section, we will show you how to use *the power of your love to reestablish your connection.* Your actions and attitudes can go a long way toward making a reconnection that will bring about attachment, intimacy, and positive feelings toward your spouse. Rescue is at hand.

> *Thank You, Lord God, that You love me even when I'm not very lovable, when I'm not very likable, and when I behave in ways that disappoint You. Thank You for Your faithful and steadfast love—and teach me to offer that kind of love to my mate. You know the times when I'd rather cut and run. At those times, help me to look to You, to know Your strength in my weakness, and to love my mate with Your love. In Jesus's name. Amen.*

Hurt Happens, But You Can Handle It

Like the folks at the marriage seminar, you need to remember that the wonderful person whom you love so much, need so much, and desire to be with so much is an imperfect person and will do things, mostly unintentionally but some very intentionally, that will hurt you. You have married a sinner who will fail you at times, and it's going to hurt. But that's OK, because the good stuff is worth all the pain.

★ Why is it freeing to see these truths in black and white?

Were you surprised the first time your beloved hurt you or failed you? Why or why not?

★ Are you expecting your mate to never hurt you or fail you? Why or why not?

Realize that not only is your mate far from ideal, and immature, but he or she *will* hurt you. The more fully you accept that reality, the better your relationship will be. Simply accept pain as part of the package.

This is a great exercise, so take time right now to do it. List some of the wonderful qualities about your mate and the reasons you married him. Focus on your lover's strengths, special things about him, and feel how you are drawn to him.

★ Are you willing to accept pain as part of this package? Why or why not? If so, what will that acceptance look like and sound like? Be specific.

_____

_____

_____

_____

False Expectations

People set themselves up for failure by expecting a good marriage to be one without pain, and that expectation comes in at least these three forms.

THE WISH FOR A CHILDHOOD FANTASY. Children dream of marrying a fantasy prince or princess who will always make his or her life fun and happy. *Marriage should be all fun*, they think. *It should always make me happy. It should not hurt.* And especially their fantasy prince or princess should not be the one to hurt them! Some partners enter marriage with this childhood fantasy. So when those hurts do come and the marriage is not fun anymore, many cut and run.

When the hurts come in our marriage, we realize that the vow "for better or for worse" is a very important one. What "worse" are you dealing with in your marriage right now? What will you do to "lean into it"?

_____

_____

_____

What will you do to love your mate the way you want to be loved even when your "worse" is the issue at hand?

_____

_____

_____

THE WISH FOR A PAIN-FREE LIFE. No matter how much you wish it were otherwise, the reality is that we live in a fallen world, and bad things happen.

As Jesus said, "In this world, you will have trouble" (John 16:33). People we love die. Accidents happen, and people get hurt. Financial setbacks hit us. What kind of trouble and pain have you and your lover had the opportunity to go through together?

_____

_____

_____

Did the two of you deal with the pain and lean into it together? If so, what benefits came from doing so? What new strength in your relationship did you experience?

_____

_____

_____

Did the two of you try to avoid the pain? What have been the consequences of that choice? What might you do to make yourselves and the situation available to God so that He can redeem the situation?

_____

_____

_____

THE WISH TO MAKE UP FOR PAST HURT. When the past has held substantial hurt and pain, a person may dream of a relationship that will one day make it all better, of being with a man whose love will heal all her past hurts. But even when she finds a really good relationship with a good man, he does disappoint her at times. There *are* hurts and pains, and this person experiences a double hurt—the hurt itself as well as the greater hurt of being disappointed that the longed-for rescue did not happen.

What past hurts would you have liked your spouse to make up for?

_____

_____

_____

Take that list to the Lord in prayer. He is the one and only Source of true healing. Pray, too, about any impact your "wish-to-make-up-for-past-hurt" expectation has had on your marriage.

_____

_____

_____

The Reality

Each and every one of us will hurt each other, even the people we love the most. We all get it wrong sometimes, and that will often cause hurt. Partners in good marriages realize this, and as a result they develop the following attitudes and practices that preserve the connection, even when one has hurt the other.

ACCEPT THE FACT THAT YOUR MATE WILL SOMETIMES DO THINGS THAT HURT YOU. When you accept this fact, you'll be able to deal with the hurts when they come, and those hurts won't destroy the connection and the love you share.

HANG ON TO THE THINGS THAT YOU LOVE ABOUT YOUR MATE, EVEN WHEN HE DISAPPOINTS YOU. Do not label your mate as "all bad." He gets it wrong at times, of course, but he is still a wonderful creation of God with extraordinary qualities. Don't let the hurts blind you to his good qualities.

WHEN HURT HAPPENS, FACE IT WITH HONESTY AND DIRECTNESS. Partners in good marriages do not deny problems; they face them. When you are hurt, tell each other. Speak the truth, but do so in love, not anger (Ephesians 4:25–26).

WHEN YOU ARE THE ONE WHO HAS HURT THE OTHER, APOLOGIZE. Confess your wrongdoing—do not excuse it!—and empathize with the hurt you have caused. The worst thing you can do is rationalize it or explain it away. Just realize that this was one of your moments to blow it. Confess your offense, and ask for forgiveness.

WHEN YOU ARE HURT, GRIEVE IT AND FORGIVE. Forgiveness is as vital as your digestive tract. It is the way that we metabolize and remove waste from the system of a relationship.

IF THE HURT IS SEVERE, GET SUPPORT AND HEALING, AND PROCESS THE PAIN. Grieving the hurt and letting it go may be impossible without outside help if a major hurt has been inflicted.

GET STRAIGHT ABOUT WHAT IS WORTH BEING HURT OVER. Some things simply are not worth bringing up or making into an issue. If you find yourself hurt continually by much of what your mate does, you may need outside help to correct your perspective.

WORK TOGETHER ON HOW YOU PROCESS PAIN AND HURT. Talk to each other about how to let each other know when you are hurt. Discuss what you need from each other at those moments. Grow in your communication, listening, and conflict resolution skills. Take a class or a workshop. See resolving hurt and conflict as one of the most important skills that you can develop.

These are simple but not easy steps, and many of them call us to choose wisely what we think about and focus on when we are hurting. Ask for the Holy Spirit's strength and help as you deal with the reality that we all hurt each other.

_____

_____

What action steps, if any, do you think might be good to take in light of what you just read? What outside help, class, or workshop might you seek out—and when will you do so?

_____

_____

A Lifeline: YOU CAN BE MARRIED TO A PERSON WHO HURTS YOU AND YET HAVE A WONDERFUL RELATIONSHIP. THE TRIALS IN YOUR MARRIAGE AND IN LIFE WILL ONLY MAKE YOU STRONGER AND MORE MATURE IN THE END. THEY WILL BUILD YOUR CHARACTER AND MAKE YOUR RELATIONSHIP STRONGER THAN IF YOU HAD NEVER GONE THROUGH THEM. BUT THAT CAN HAPPEN ONLY IF YOU SEE HURT AS PART OF THE PACKAGE. THEN YOU WON'T BE SURPRISED, BUT EQUIPPED.

Past Hurts Present Problems

You may have heard someone say, "The light at the end of the tunnel is a train headed toward you." We're going to twist this saying into a description of something that often occurs in love relationships: There may be times when the light at the end of the tunnel really is love, but you may mistake it for a train and swerve to avoid it. When you do, the good that could have benefited you and your mate never occurs.

> What moments in your marriage, if any, come to mind as you read that analogy? Give an example.
>
> _____
>
> _____
>
> _____
>
> In that situation, why do you think you swerved to avoid what looked like a train?
>
> _____
>
> _____
>
> _____

Swerving to avoid what looks like a train can mean the loss of many satisfying, intimate, and enjoyable times of love and connection. Missing out on those good things may seem dumb, but it can happen to the best of us. We'll explain all this and show how you can recognize the true light of love for what it is and not try to dodge it.

A Good Marriage Transfers Love

Just as a good cell phone transfers information, a good marriage will transfer love. And that love has many voices, many ways to be heard and received. It can be the voice of grace, affection, comfort, compassion, need, encouragement, or passion, to name a few. The "voice" is not always audible; it can come in many forms—a glance, a word, a conversation, or a touch. Even though love comes our way, we all have a tendency to misunderstand what our mate wants to provide for us. And we often swerve out of the way, causing disconnection, alienation, and hurt between two good people who actually do love each other.

When has your lover misunderstood what you wanted to provide for him?

_____

_____

_____

When have you misunderstood what your lover wanted to provide for you?

_____

_____

_____

What, if anything, did you understand at the time about why you or he swerved out of the way of love?

_____

_____

_____

Why would we avoid the very thing that we desire and need from our lover? In a nutshell, we miss the voice of love in our spouse because old messages drown it out. Past hurts and unresolved issues can distort the true meaning and emotion that is coming your way in your marriage.

Is It Love, or Is It a Train?

Think back on how Debbie and Kevin's connection was affected when Kevin perceived the light of Debbie's love to be a train.

What old message from Kevin's past drowned out Debbie's love?

What question did Debbie ask Kevin to help him see that he was swerving away from her love?

★ What help or encouragement does Kevin and Debbie's situation offer you?

Get to Know Your "Train"

There are other "trains at the end of the tunnel" besides Debbie and Kevin's. See if any of the following is a train in your life.

IF YOU TELL ME THE TRUTH, YOU DON'T LOVE ME. This feeling could be due to past experiences of harsh judgment with little compassion.

IF YOU COME CLOSE, YOU WILL DRAIN ME. This reaction often results from a family system in which a child had to take care of the dependency needs of a parent.

LOVE MEANS CONTROL. Any form of intimacy is experienced as a way to tie him down, and he must escape by distancing.

YOU'LL LEAVE ME. One spouse has suffered abandonment by someone she loved, and she has learned not to trust in the goodness and stability of love.

Think about your past. Which one of these trains, if any, do you think might be coming down the track toward you?

Knowing what you do of your lover's past, which one of these trains, if any, might she be worried about or even expecting to come her way?

The Bottom Line

The bottom line is this: *couples committed to rescuing their love life will search for, identify, and deal with whatever is getting in the way of the voice of love.* They won't tolerate old hurts from the past screwing up the opportunity for full, rich, and exciting love for the rest of their lives.

What past hurts do you need to address so that they don't interfere with your present connection?

★ What does the reference to bacterial infection and antibiotics tell you about those past hurts?

_____

_____

_____

Learning to Hear the Voice of Love

Here are some good things you can do as a couple to administer the right antibiotics.

DISCUSS RESPONSES THAT DON'T MAKE SENSE. Talk to each other about any times when one of you approached the other with a good and positive message, but your spouse withdrew, shut down, felt hurt, or became irritated. Explain what your intent was and help the other person discover the source of the reaction. *Don't be satisfied with simply identifying the reaction.*

UNEARTH THE PATTERNS. Using the examples in this chapter as a starting point, help each other discover what sorts of patterns you have as a couple that get in the way of love, connection, and passion. Is one of you afraid the other will leave? Is one still struggling with childhood abandonment? Is one still attempting to protect her freedom from her parents? Get to know the patterns.

VALIDATE EACH OTHER'S EXPERIENCE. Don't say to each other, "I'm not your dad; get over it." Instead, say something like, "I understand that when I confront you, it's hard for you to feel that I love you at the same time. I know those feelings are real, and I don't want to make it worse for you." Validation helps your spouse see that you are different from her past experiences. You are not a train; you are a true lover.

SEPARATE PAST FROM PRESENT. You and your mate

need to help each other make a distinction between the old and the new, so that you can hear each other's voices of love. Say, "I want you to know that when I do confront you, I am not wanting to hurt or control you. I just want to solve a problem so we can get back to being close and safe for each other."

SET UP FEEDBACK. Memories of past injuries and issues need to be addressed over a process of time and given the right ingredients of love, safety, and reality. So give each other permission to bring up the "train" when one of you notices it. That helps to break the grip of the past on your present connection.

STAY IN CONFESSION. You and your mate may sometimes truly be "trains" for each other. In these instances, don't hide or pretend. Confess your negative behavior and tell the truth. Confession is good for the soul, and the marriage.

★ Comment on these prescribed antibiotics—on the wisdom, their potential, and how doable they seem.

_____

_____

_____

What recent "train" do you need to talk to your lover about? Plan and pray, asking God to both guide your words and help you hear the voice of love.

_____

_____

_____

A Lifeline: HELP EACH OTHER NOT TO SWERVE AND AVOID LOVE WHEN IT COMES YOUR WAY.

Accepting Without Approving

Dan and Stephanie had come a long way since the early days when he had seemed so critical and unaccepting. But after a lot of talking about it, Stephanie remembered, "I finally realized that it wasn't about accepting me. It was about expecting things of me. I saw those two things as the same. But I finally got it that they were different, and things got better."

In what ways, if any, are you—or might you seem—unaccepting of your lover?

_____

_____

When, if at all, do you feel unaccepted by your lover?

_____

_____

Explain how, if at all, you or your lover may be confusing acceptance and expectations.

_____

_____

_____

Acceptance and Love

Acceptance is a term often used to mean your love is so great and so deep nothing the two of you can do will really disturb or distance each other, and all can be forgiven and forgotten in the service of love. But there is more to acceptance than that.

When we accept someone, we receive that person into our heart. We take in all parts, all aspects, all realities, good, bad, and green. In response to the acceptance God gives to us, we "accept one another, then, just as Christ accepted you, in order to bring praise to God" (Romans 15:7).

★ Why does it make sense that we can't love, trust, or grow without knowing that we have been received, warts and all, by another person?

_____

_____

_____

When have you felt you had to earn acceptance? Explain why that felt—or didn't feel—like genuine acceptance.

_____

_____

_____

If you have to earn it or be good enough, by definition it cannot be acceptance. Acceptance is based on the acceptor's love and the acceptee's need. It has nothing to do with performance, working hard enough, or being good enough.

★ The two enemies of acceptance in a connection are *denial* and *judgment*. Why is each of those an enemy of acceptance?

_____

_____

_____

★Needs and weaknesses are usually at the top of the list of those things a couple should learn to accept in each other. But we can't accept each other's faults and failings, immaturities, and undesirable habits if we're denying that they even exist. Besides, acceptance and love are the only way that those parts of you two will ever have a chance to grow, heal, change, and mature. When, if ever, has the sense of being accepted empowered you to take steps to grow, heal, change, or mature?

All growth begins with acceptance, for without it we just hide and pretend better, hoping to avoid the disappointment and wrath of our partner. Only in the light and freedom of acceptance can you talk about, process, pray, support, and come up with solutions for these weaknesses and issues.

Approval and Agreement

Now let's set out what acceptance is *not*. A major misconception about acceptance is that it conveys approval or agreement. The thinking generally goes something like, *If you don't approve of or agree with what I am doing, you aren't accepting me.* This is not true, and it doesn't work in relationships.

When have you accepted a person but not approved of or agreed with that person's action, speech, or attitude?

What did you do for the person, if anything, to differen-
tiate between accepting the person and not approving of
her words or behavior?

_____

_____

_____

Do you think that person felt accepted even though you
didn't approve of or agree with her action, speech, or
attitude? Why or why not?

_____

_____

_____

What does this scenario you've been thinking about
suggest for how to approach your lover with acceptance
but not approval?

_____

_____

_____

If you approve of or agree with something that is bad, immature, or wrong, you are contributing to more of the same,
which is what you will most likely experience. You shouldn't
approve of what could be bad for you as a couple.

Feeling Attacked

Some people respond to disapproval by feeling hated, judged,
and persecuted. Psychologists call this a *persecutory issue*, and
it stems from a person's character and experiences in significant relationships.

Is it possible that your spouse has a persecutory issue to some degree? Why or why not?

_____

_____

_____

What from his past might be behind that issue?

_____

_____

_____

If confronting a problem you disapprove of destroys your partner's sense of acceptance, work on it with her. Make it a project. Reassure her that you love her. Get other healthy people to help her see that you love her. Help her be aware of past hurts and old patterns that may be causing her reactions, so they can be resolved. Be as accepting, humble, loving, and open as you can be. But whatever you do, *do not give up your position,* as long as it is healthy and reasonable. You want growth and improvement. To love and accept each other totally, you must care enough to confront.

A Lifeline: DISAPPROVAL AND ACCEPTANCE SEEM MUTUALLY EXCLUSIVE, BUT THEY ARE NOT. IF YOU WANT TO RESCUE YOUR LOVE LIFE, START BY TOTALLY ACCEPTING AND RECEIVING EVERY ASPECT OF EACH OTHER WITHOUT DENIAL OR JUDGMENT. THEN BRING UP TO THE LIGHT FOR DISCUSSION AND CHANGE THOSE BEHAVIORS AND ATTITUDES THAT BLOCK YOUR LOVE FROM EACH OTHER.

Lovers Can Bring Out the Worst in Each Other

You've probably noticed that *your closest relationship can also be your most difficult relationship.*

★ When have you experienced this undeniable reality? Give a specific example or two.

★ Closely related, when has a simple phrase or a certain look from your mate profoundly affected your emotions, especially the negative ones? What was the trigger—and what was triggered? Did you feel criticized, misunder- stood, unloved, like an idiot, or something else?

You can experience both the best and the worst of emotions in your connection with this delightful but exasperating person. Marilyn experienced that in her relationship with Jeff—and she observed that *it only started happening when they got more serious.* The deeper the connection becomes, the more problems you and your partner will encounter.

Making Sense of the Problem

You would think that the closer you get to someone you love, the better things should be. Increased time, vulnerability, experience, and love should lead to increased trust, desire, and satisfaction, right? But increased closeness can also bring out dark, intimacy-breaking issues. Let's take a look at how this happens.

LOVE REGRESSES US. As you become safer and more vulnerable, you expose parts of yourself that don't normally come out in everyday life. God designed love to bring out vulnerable parts of us at their proper time. Then, if the relationship is safe enough, you can expose your fragile and vulnerable parts to get the grace, caring, and empathy that you need.

When have you experienced a degree of regression in a relationship? Share some details.

When have you sensed your mate experiencing a degree of regression in your relationship?

Reflect on this statement: "Regression is a good sign. *If love regresses you, you are alive and allowing yourself to be connected at deep levels.*" How will this truth help you stay connected?

OLD PATTERNS ARE REENACTED. Not only do we regress in our deepest love relationship, but we also reenact old patterns that we haven't resolved.

An example of this is one person playing the "lover" and the other, the "fighter." These are roles that many learned in order to survive their families of origin. Do you and your spouse experience the lover/fighter pattern? If so, what from your past is the pattern rooted in?

_____

_____

_____

What other patterns from your past, if any, have been reenacted in your relationship? What circumstances and/or relationships were those patterns rooted in?

_____

_____

_____

CLOSENESS BRINGS FEAR. Many times, the very presence of closeness and vulnerability can elicit strong feelings of fear and distancing.

For either of you, has closeness meant being hurt, controlled, or abandoned? In what ways has that history affected—or does it affect—your connection?

_____

_____

As love penetrates the heart at a deeper level, _whatever is there gets activated_—including conflicts, fears, immaturity, unresolved trauma, and the like. What experience with this reality have you had in your marriage? Be specific.

_____

_____

_____

CLOSENESS PROVIDES AMMUNITION. When you expose yourself to the other person, you give her information about yourself that, unfortunately, she can use against you.

Why is this a sign of immaturity?

_____

_____

_____

Why is the natural response—retaliating in kind with what you know about the person who hurt you—also a sign of immaturity?

_____

_____

_____

Bringing Out the Best in the Worst

Bringing out the worst in each other is an inevitable problem that can sink your love life. It's dumb not to recognize it and deal with it—and we have some simple and straightforward solutions for you. But first, remember that if you two are disconnected because the relationship brings out the worst in you, it's a sign that *the relationship matters*. It is powerful enough to make you a little crazy, and that is good news. Here are some things you can do to reestablish the satisfying connection you need.

AFFIRM THE LIFE. In a quiet and peaceful period, not in the throes of battle, talk with each other about the reality that there is a lot of care and love between you. Simply recognizing and confessing how much you matter to each other ("I don't let anyone make me as crazy as you do. You must be pretty special to me!") can bring a sense of being valued and loved.

MAKE IT RELATIONAL. When one of you brings out the worst in the other, *make the issue part of the relationship itself, because it truly is part of who you are as a couple.* Bring into the light what is already true about you, and talk about it. Doing so can lead to understanding and mutuality.

STRENGTHEN THE WEAK PARTS. When you become aware of what things "get to you" in the relationship, it is a signal to shore up, develop, and strengthen those parts. Those things are often a symptom of some sort of brokenness or injury within, so work on healing and growth.

GIVE YOUR BEST TO THE RELATIONSHIP. It is very easy, as you become more used to each other, to take each other for granted and strut your good stuff only when you're with others. Make your relationship one in which your first thought is to give the best, healthiest, and most adult parts of your heart to your lover.

HONOR YOUR COMMITMENT. When your mate exposes the worst of himself and you are tempted to break your marriage vows, you must go through reality and make a choice to love. The commitment of marriage not only protects us from bailing out when the inevitable comes, but it also ensures that we truly do get to the promised land of real intimacy and love.

★ Comment on these five steps. Do you find them doable, if not entirely comfortable?

....

....

....

Which of these five steps, if any, would you be wise to take sooner rather than later? Be specific about, for instance, what you will do to "strengthen the weak parts" or to "give your best to the relationship."

_____

_____

_____

A Lifeline: FACE IT: YOUR LOVE CONNECTION WILL BRING OUT THE WORST IN YOU, WHICH SIMPLY MEANS THAT LOVE IS TAKING ITS NORMAL PATH. REMEMBER THAT THIS IS A VITAL SIGN OF LIFE, AND BRING IT INTO YOUR LOVE LIFE WHERE YOU CAN ADDRESS IT SQUARELY, HELPING EACH OTHER TO GROW AND CHANGE. REMEMBER YOUR MARRIAGE VOWS, AND WORK IT THROUGH WITH PATIENCE AND GRACE.

Resist the Temptation to Cut and Run

While you were hypothetically sitting in the counselor's chair, you heard some very typical words from people who have had affairs or have considered affairs (Book pgs. 121–122).

★ What were your initial thoughts to these statements?

_____

_____

_____

A Common Thread

Did you notice the common thread in these complaints? Each person thought the affair happened because their mates did not meet their needs. Oh, there is truth to the claim that things were not going well in the relationship before the affair. Their spouses were not giving them all that they needed, or at least wanted. But that is not why they had the affair. *They had the affair because they chose to solve their misery in that particular way.*

Why can't we cast the first stone against these folks who had an affair? See Romans 3:23.

What insight into the dynamics behind an affair did you gain from this discussion?

The key issue here is not guilt or condemnation; it is getting to the real disease behind infidelity. First, we need to understand that deprivation is not what causes failure. Deprivation may provide the motivation to look for comfort, even illicitly. But it does not cause the choice to achieve comfort in a destructive way. Jesus knew deprivation. Yet when temptation came to answer his deprivation, He did not go the way of immediate comfort. He denied that option. James tells us that we sin because we are carried away by our own desires (James 1:14–15).

Deprivation, stress, hurt, and need are not to be dealt with by things that cause death. What kinds of death does infidelity cause?

_____

_____

_____

We want your relationship to be "affair-proofed" so that you can avoid these kinds of death. Technically, "affair-proofing" is impossible, because no human is above any temptation. But certain attitudes can bring your chances of falling much closer to zero.

Dissatisfaction Is *Your* Problem

While your mate's behavior may be the cause of your dissatisfaction, your *response* is your responsibility. And you are the only one who can choose your response. You have the freedom to do the right and helpful thing in response to your spouse's failure. Your response can be a redemptive force for change in your marriage instead of a force to take it further down. As Jesus said, even "sinners" love the people who love them.

The real test is how well we love someone who does not love us well. That is the true calling of Christ. Here is how he says it: "If you love those who love you, what credit is that to you? Even 'sinners' love those who love them. And if you do good to those who are good to you, what credit is that to you? Even 'sinners' do that" (Luke 6:32–33).

Who will support you in your efforts to respond responsibly and not destructively to dissatisfaction in your marriage?

_____

What reinforcement for this course of action do you find in Jesus's words and example?

_____

_____

_____

As we said earlier, you should not just endure mistreatment. In fact, the loving thing to do is to take a stand against the mistreatment and confront it in a loving and redemptive way. The loving thing is to make the effort to do what is necessary to turn things around. Sometimes that means you may have to take some tough growth steps yourself in order to do it correctly.

Your feelings of being alone and hurt are very real and need help. Where will you go to find help and healing?

_____

_____

_____

Affairs are not healing. They are destructive, like illegal drugs. The responsible thing to do is take your pain to good people who can love you, support you, and help you through the process of healing your marriage.

Attraction Is a Bad Barometer

First of all, attraction is based on becoming intoxicated by someone with whom they do not have a real and whole relationship, and they idealize the part of him that they relate to. Second, affairs are so attractive because they offer a partial relationship that only includes the positive. An idealized, "all-good" fantasy is allowed to remain intact because it does not have the day-to-day pressures that marriage inevitably has. So the hurt spouse has an inordinately positive view of the rescuer, which he or she mistakes for love.

What role does the fantasy versus reality conflict play in affairs? In the high divorce rate of second marriages?

Review some of the truths about fantasy that we discussed in Dumb Attitude #3 (Book pgs. 70–73).

If you are attracted to someone strongly enough to consider an affair, heed the warning of Solomon about infidelity: "For the lips of an adulteress drip honey, and her speech is smoother than oil; but in the end she is bitter as gall, sharp as a double-edged sword. Her feet go down to death; her steps lead straight to the grave" (Proverbs 5:3–5).

Think about not only the captivating romantic scene of your fantasy affair. Play the movie all the way to its tragic end (Book pg. 125). When have you seen this played out in real life? Consider yourself warned!

Before you raise the lights and lock the theater doors for the night, add another scene to the plot: the one where you get smart and run the other way. Do not succumb to the fantasy of attraction.

Adultery Is Not About Your Needs

Too often, people claim that they were driven into an affair because their mate did not meet their needs in some way. Related to that is the feeling many people have that they deserve to have their needs met. It is their "right" to get what they want or need in life.

People who have successful lives and relationships hold to a different philosophy. Instead of thinking of themselves as entitled to what they want, they believe that their God and the people they make commitments to are entitled to having them live up to the standards they hold to.

Toward which end of the spectrum do you lean? Do you feel entitled to have your needs met, or do you recognize that people you've made commitments to (e.g., your spouse) are entitled to have you live up to those commitments? Support your answer with evidence from your life.

_____

_____

_____

The paradox is that when we hold to those standards and commitments, we are the ones who get what we most want in life. We suffer through the hard times in order to resolve problems and make relationships last. When things are tough, our first thought is not about how our needs are not being met, but about what we can do to redeem the relationship.

★ This very countercultural truth is exactly what Jesus modeled for us: dying to yourself and picking up your cross (Matthew 16:24). What opportunities—big and small—does your marriage give you to die to yourself?

_____

_____

★ To redeem bad things, we sometimes have to suffer not getting what we need, just as Jesus suffered. But good suffering always produces good results. When have you seen that truth in real life? Start your list by looking at the cross.

_____

_____

Whenever you feel that your need is becoming more urgent than your values, what should that signal for you and what course of action should it suggest?

_____

_____

_____

We'll answer that question for you: it means that you have a real and important need for love and relationship that is going unmet. Instead of letting that need drive you into an affair, turn to your godly, supportive friends and relationships to meet that need while you work on your marriage. It will pay off for you in the long run.

Clearly, "for better or for worse"—the vow you took—is a serious vow and a hard one, especially when your needs are unmet. But if you make your commitment more important than your need, you have the greatest chance of reaping the fruit that those values were designed to bring about.

When the Wolf Knocks, Don't Open the Door

One of the most common dumb attitudes is the confidence in our own will power to resist temptation. (If you don't believe it, look at your dieting history.) We humans think we are stronger than we really are, but given the right circumstances—ploys by the devil, our own dependencies, and other factors—we are all subject to falling to some kind of temptation, including the temptation to infidelity. As the Bible teaches, pride does go before a fall, and we are most vulnerable when we think we are strong enough to stand (Proverbs 16:18; 1 Corinthians 10:12).

Do you honestly think you are strong enough to stand against temptation and the devil?

What accountability have you built—or will you build—into your life? With whom will you choose to be totally honest about your marriage so that that person can hold you accountable to your vows, help you when needs are not being met in your marriage, and pray for you during your marriage's stormy times? Have couple's accountability as well. Keeping out of temptation keeps you out of trouble.

Avoid even opening the door to temptation. The Bible does not say to resist temptation; it says to "flee" from the devil, who is the author of temptation (1 Corinthians 6:18). If you place yourself in a tempting situation and rely on your moral strength to resist it, you are asking for trouble. Don't rely on a strategy to resist the temptations the devil puts in your path, but avoid placing yourself in them to begin with. As Mark Twain said, "It's easier to stay out than to get out." In what past situation do you wish you had heeded this advice? Let that be a word of warning to you, a word that compels you to flee the devil and his efforts to tempt you to sin.

Only you know when you may be tempted and when you won't. There are too many variables for us to tell you what you should and should not do. But you know.

Where have you drawn the line between what is acceptable and what isn't?

Have you talked about those lines with your lover—and heeded her feelings of comfort or discomfort?

Neither of you should be doing things the other feels uncomfortable with. Talk it through and avoid any kind of duplicity.

A Lifeline: KNOW THAT IF THE LEAST BIT OF THE OPPORTUNITY FOR TEMPTATION APPEARS, THAT IS THE WOLF. WHEN HE FINDS YOU ALONE, HE WILL EAT YOU. THE LONE SHEEP IS THE ONE WHO ALWAYS GETS ATTACKED. SO STAY ON THE PATH WITH THE REST OF THE FLOCK, AND AVOID BEING ALONE WITH THE WOLF OF TEMPTATION. WHENEVER HE KNOCKS, DO NOT OPEN THE DOOR.

Living What I Learn

Which of this section's four topics did you find most relevant or helpful? Explain.

❑ Hurt Happens, But You Can Handle It
❑ Past Hurts Present Problems
❑ Accepting Without Approving
❑ Lovers Can Bring Out the Worst in Each Other
❑ Resist the Temptation to Cut and Run

_____

_____

_____

★ Share one or two insights from the text that you found especially encouraging.

_____

_____

_____

Which of the following lifelines will you grab this week?

❑ Realize that hurt is part of the package. Then you'll be equipped—not surprised—when it comes.

❑ Help each other not to swerve and avoid love when it comes your way.

❑ Rescue your love life by totally accepting and receiving every aspect of each other without denial or judgment *and* by bringing up to the light for discussion and change those behaviors and attitudes that block your love from each other.

❑ Your love connection can bring out the worst in you. Remember that this is a vital sign of life, and bring it into your love life where you can address it squarely, helping each other to grow and change.

❑ Avoid being alone with the wolf of temptation. Whenever he knocks, do not open the door.

What specific step(s) will you take to help rescue yourself and thereby rescue your marriage?

_____

_____

_____

As you close in prayer, ask God to help you love with His love the person He has given you as a spouse, a person He sent His Son to die for. Ask Him also to grant you wisdom to recognize when the lights are love and not a train, discernment regarding good pain versus bad pain, courage to address problems and to flee temptation, and people to hold you accountable to your vows.

When you go to the meeting, be ready to . . .

• SHARE YOUR ANSWERS TO THE STARRED (★) QUESTIONS.

• CHOOSE WHICH OF THE LIFELINES YOU'LL GRAB AND WORK ON THIS WEEK.

During the week . . .

• AS YOU WORK ON YOUR SECTION 4 LIFELINE, PAY ATTENTION TO THE EFFECTS OF YOUR EFFORTS ON YOU, ON YOUR MATE, AND ON YOUR MARRIAGE.

DUMB ATTITUDE #5

"My Lover Should Read My Mind"

Establishing, preserving and repairing the connection is essential in a relationship. And to do that requires being able to communicate. That means being able to talk to one another in a way that gets the two of you closer instead of farther apart. Sadly, because we are human, that is a very difficult thing to do at times.

Have you ever been accused of saying things you didn't mean? If so, what was that experience like?

_____

_____

Have you ever been upset with your partner for not being able to figure out why you were angry with him? If so, how able was your spouse to read your mind? Was this an effective way to communicate with him?

_____

Comment on the frequency of such disconnects in your relationship with your lover. What tends to cause such interactions? What pattern, if any, have you noticed in the precipitating circumstances? What side of the conversation do you tend to find yourself on?

What follows are some very "learnable" principles about how to talk to each other and how *not* to talk to each other as well as about how to listen to each other in some ways that you may never have done. If you follow these principles, you won't ever again fall for the dumb attitude of expecting your partner to read your mind.

Lord God, you are the Master Communicator. Help me give myself sacrificially to the effort to communicate my love, my heart, and my feelings to my mate. Please teach me to listen to feelings and not just words; to listen with my heart and not just my ears. Please help me recognize when I'm hearing things that aren't being said—and when things I'm not saying are being heard! And please help me take the steps I need to take—steps of faith—to communicate clearly and to strengthen this marriage that You've ordained. In Jesus's name. Amen.

Don't Hide Your Feelings

You probably know the experience of being surprised that someone close to you felt a certain way, and you had no clue. It happens in a marriage! Sometimes one partner doesn't hear when the other is trying to communicate something important. But at other times the communication is not so clear after all.

★ When has your mate been surprised about your feelings when you thought you were communicating quite clearly?

When have you been completely surprised by your mate's feelings—once you finally realized what those feelings were?

Why People Hide Their Feelings

Something happens to the openness and intimacy of a relationship's early seasons. The two people slowly stop communicating what they *really* think and feel, and they slowly get further and further away from each other emotionally. Why did the sharing stop and the detachment set in?

★ Which of the following reasons (explained more fully on Book pgs. 130–132) have been factors in your marriage?

❑ You've learned that, in your marriage, sharing is not safe.

❑ You have old fears—from before you were married—that keep you from sharing.

❑ You do not have the skills or know how to share.

❑ You have had experiences that are too overwhelming.

❑ You feel that the things that you want to share are unacceptable.

❑ You think that your desires or wants are not important.

Whatever your reason, hiding your feelings is not only dishonest, but it's a dumb attitude that can sink a marriage in a sea of lies and miscommunication. If this is your problem, you can do something about it. And it's not as hard as you think—read on!

Whatever the Reason, You Can Turn It Around

If you want to rescue your love life and reestablish connection, you have to start sharing. Here are some tips on how to reestablish your connection.

STOP LYING.

If this is a problem for you, what are you trying to avoid by lying?

What does it mean to you that countless spouses have said that they wish they could just have the truth, no matter how bad it is, instead of lies?

STOP FUDGING.

If this is a problem for you, what are you trying to avoid by fudging?

_____

_____

What does it mean to you that, for the sake of keeping the peace and togetherness, people fudge on how they really feel and what they really think and, as a result, lose both peace and togetherness?

_____

_____

_____

BE DIRECT.

If being direct doesn't come easily, why do you think it's such a struggle for you?

_____

_____

Which of the following do you need to learn to say— and with whom will you practice?

❏ "I want . . ."
❏ "I think . . ."
❏ "I don't like it when . . ."
❏ "I don't want . . ."
❏ "I feel . . ."
❏ "I hate . . ."
❏ "I like . . ."
❏ "I prefer . . .

FACE YOUR FEARS.

If you are not direct and honest, what might you be afraid of?

_____

_____

That fear may be keeping you from doing what would be much better for you and your relationship in the end. Face those fears—and what exactly would "facing that fear" look like? Be specific.

_____

_____

_____

SAY MORE WITH LESS.

Do you tend to be wordy rather than concise and direct? If so, why?

_____

_____

If so, practice saying whatever you want to say in one-third the number of words. Learning to simply begin with "I think . . ." or "I want . . ." can make connection possible.

_____

_____

_____

LET YOUR MATE HAVE HER OWN REACTION.

You cannot control your mate's reaction. You are not responsible for it, and you cannot allow your fear of his or her reaction turn you into a liar. What specific reaction(s) do you especially fear—and in what might that fear be rooted?

_____

_____

_____

What will you do to counter that fear? What truth can you speak to yourself?

_____

_____

_____

ADDRESS THE REASONS YOU CAN'T TALK.

Is your relationship unable to handle honesty? Is there just not enough grace in the relationship to face the truth?

_____

_____

_____

If you answered yes to either or both of those questions, what can you do to address that issue so that your relationship can get to the place where honesty can happen?

_____

_____

_____

Is timing the reason you can't talk? If so, what will you do to strengthen the relationship while you're waiting until the proper time to share something really painful or waiting to confront the spouse until she is ready to hear?

_____

_____

_____

In most situations, the issue is not about honesty threatening the whole relationship. It is more about honesty causing fights and disconnects. If that is your issue, talk about why you can't talk (see Book pg. 135 for some guidelines and possibilities). Begin with the question, "What do I do to make it hard for you to be honest with me?" Then listen to what you hear.

_____

_____

_____

MAKE THE PROBLEM THE PROBLEM, NOT THE PERSON.

Do you practice this key principle? Talk about the issue, or the problem, or the thing that you do not like, instead of smearing the character and personhood of your partner in the process. Give specific evidence in support of your answer.

_____

_____

_____

★Address a specific problem in concise language that conveys helpful information. Why will doing so make your relationship work better?

Right now practice being specific and concise about one or two real-life situations in your marriage. Then you'll be ready when that situation arises.

To Know and Be Known

People in good relationships process things continually. Also, good relationships can handle realities like aloneness, dissatisfaction, temptation, and financial struggle. In fact, research shows that the best relationships are the ones where couples go *toward each other with the most difficult things.*

Is communication in your relationship more like a DSL line or a dial-up system? Explain your answer.

When, if ever, has something good happened as you and your spouse went toward each other in the face of a difficult reality? Be specific about the reality as well as about the "something good."

A Lifeline: IN GOOD RELATIONSHIPS, TALKING IS HONEST AND FREE OF HEDGING, HIDING FEELINGS, AND NUANCES. THESE COUPLES LIVE THE TRUTH OF SOLOMON: "AN HONEST ANSWER IS LIKE A KISS ON THE LIPS" (PROVERBS 24:26). WHEN THEY DO THAT, THEY FIND THAT THE KISSES ON THE LIPS TEND TO BE A LOT BETTER TOO!

Choose to Face Reality

Christy and Brian's lunch out with their kids took an unexpected turn when Sophie needed to be disciplined. Sparks flew, and Brian was frustrated. He felt as if he could not discuss issues with Christy, as if he couldn't bring anything up without her reacting. Brian felt stuck, and Christy felt as alone as he did.

Before the conflict, Brian and Christy were feeling close to one another and having a great time as a family. What happened? Was there a dumb attitude here on the part of either of them? One that could have sunk their love life?

The Need for Both Love and Reality

Christy and Brian were feeling very loving and together before the incident, but behind that lurked a reality problem that was undermining a lot of the love they shared. The reality was the kids needed discipline, Christy felt that Brian criticized her and put her down, and Brian was concerned that the kids were getting a classic "good parent–bad parent" split. He knew that they needed to obey Christy as well as him in order to grow up secure.

★ What realities in your own life are making it difficult to maintain love?

_____

_____

_____

What realities in your mate's life are making it difficult to maintain love?

_____

_____

_____

★ The realities you just listed undoubtedly affect both of you, but what other realities that you two face together are making it difficult to maintain love?

_____

_____

_____

Every day, a million couples confront the problem of facing reality and maintaining love while they do it. What causes so many people to lose their connection is that when they focus on loving each other, they do not face the harder realities they need to deal with.

★ When, if ever, have you experienced this disconnect with your spouse because you weren't facing life's "harder realities"? Was it a conscious decision? Explain.

_____

_____

_____

Another reason people lose their connection is that, when they do face life's hard realities, they don't do it in a loving way. They do it with contempt, anger, guilt, shame, condemnation, a critical spirit, blame, put-downs, sarcasm, indirectness, and a host of other ways that break the connection.

Conversely, when—if ever—have you faced life's harder realities, but not done so in a loving way? Why was it hard to be loving in that situation?

_____

_____

_____

Couples must have a way to face reality and maintain love at the same time.

Grace and Truth: The Absence of Judgment

The Bible's solution for combining love and reality is to speak the truth in love (Ephesians 4:15). Doing so combines grace and truth. *Grace* means "favor," and truth is what is—reality. This means that a couple must face the realities that they need to face, but with an attitude that keeps the other person in a position of favor. Grace is the opposite of judgment. While judgment is *against* the other person, grace is *for* her.

When bringing up a problem—a reality—assure your mate that you are on the same side; you are not against him, but for him. Speak without judgment, hurtful anger, put-downs, outbursts of rage, shame, sarcasm, or condemnation. Which of these behaviors come all too easily to you? Make it a topic of confession, repentance, and prayer.

_____

In Brian and Christy's relationship, the discipline problem was an issue to solve, not a connection breaker. It was not really about them and their love for each other, but just a child-rearing reality to negotiate. But because of the way it was communicated, the issue turned into something about their relationship instead of about the kids. *The communication itself became the problem.*

In what recent situation in your marriage would you have liked to address a tense moment as an issue to solve rather than having the conversation turn into something about your relationship? Give an example.

Now practice. What could you have said to focus on the issue that you needed to resolve? Be careful to state it in ways that are loving, not adversarial. Then the problem remains the problem, and the couple remains a team focused on solving it.

Practice again. What might you say in a hypothetical—but entirely conceivable—situation in your marriage? Imagine a decision to be made, a stressful financial situation, or child-rearing issue like Christy and Brian faced.

_____

_____

The attitude necessary to maintain the connection is one of facing reality, of communicating the issue in love with care and regard for the other person. As Paul says, "Do not let any unwholesome talk come out of your mouths, but only what is helpful for building others up according to their needs, that it may benefit those who listen. . . . Get rid of all bitterness, rage and anger, brawling and slander, along with every form of malice. Be kind and compassionate to one another" (Ephesians 4:29, 31–32).

Watch how you talk to each other when facing tough realities. Be honest with yourself. Do you speak with anger? Malice? Sarcasm? Condemnation? A critical spirit? Or do you speak in a way that is "helpful for building others up according to their needs, that it may benefit those who listen"?

_____

_____

_____

Remember the way Brian could have spoken to Christy? "It looks like you are feeling alone in disciplining our kids. Let's figure out a good way to do this. I want to help you, and also I want them to see the limits as coming from both of us. Let's talk about how to do that." Put yourself in Christy's place. What would you appreciate about Brian's words?

_____

_____

_____

The key to focusing on the issue instead of making a situation cause for disconnect is to move to connect with grace first and then talk about the tough reality. Review the tips and corresponding examples (Book pgs. 141–142).

- Affirm your spouse first.
- Listen to your spouse's perspective before giving yours.
- Listen to your own emotion in what you are saying.
- Affirm the issue that you are talking about as an important part of your relationship.
- If your emotions keep you from saying what needs to be said in a loving way, take a time-out.
- Don't use distancing language.
- Keep the goal in mind, which is not merely to look at the reality, but to preserve the connection above all else.
- Listen and take in your mate's perspective.

Which of these tips will be easy for you to follow?

_____

_____

Which of these tips will be hardest for you to do? Who can pray for you and/or hold you accountable?

_____

_____

_____

A Lifeline: LOVE AND REALITY CAN—AND MUST—GO TOGETHER TO PRESERVE YOUR CONNECTION, AND ACTING ON THE EIGHT TIPS FOR CONNECTING FIRST WITH GRACE CAN HELP.

Are You Saying What You Really Mean?

Whenever couples open their mouths, *something* happens—for better or worse. That's why it's important, when thinking about talking to your spouse, to—as business management expert Stephen Covey puts it—begin with the end in mind. Weigh each word carefully for its ultimate effect on the outcome. What are you trying to accomplish when you say that?

Remember the passage from the Book of James (Book pg.143)? What image about the power of the tongue did you find most striking?

_____

_____

When have you exercised the tongue's power of life for your lover's benefit?

_____

_____

When, recently, have you exercised the tongue's power of death at your lover's expense? Apologize and ask forgiveness.

_____

_____

_____

If you want to be understood by your spouse, then you have to choose the words and tones that will bring you that result.

If words or phrases creep in that cause your spouse to resist or become defensive or hostile, what deeper agenda inside yourself may be affecting your communication?

_____

_____

_____

_____

Let's review those few tips that will increase the likelihood of your being understood by your mate.

Seek Connection, Not Alienation

Simply put, whatever you must talk about, seek maintaining the connection as the highest goal. So think before you speak. Will what you are going to say accomplish that goal? Will it make your mate see that she is loved and cared about? Or will it somehow drive her away?

What might help you do a better job thinking before you speak?

_____

_____

_____

What role might prayer and/or the Holy Spirit play?

_____

_____

_____

Seek to Be Known

At the heart of relationship is the concept of being known.

KNOW WHAT YOU FEEL AND WANT. To make yourself known means you must first know yourself—what you feel, think, want, desire, fear, or want to communicate. And that's not always easy. Think about Sharon and Tony's conversation. He did not want to hurt her, but he had never really understood that he did. He just had seen her anger, not her hurt or fear or vulnerability. She had never shown him those things deep inside that allowed herself to be known.

What recurring issue(s) do you face in your marriage?

_____

_____

Choose one of those situations to think about. What are you really feeling in that situation? What do you really want? Is it really more money to spend? Or more time at the basketball court? Or is it really something deeper, like more respect, or freedom, or feeling like you are not controlled? What do you really want your mate to know about you?

_____

_____

_____

Learn from Sharon's negative example. Know what you really feel, and communicate it in ways that are not critical of your mate. Your vulnerability is key.

Talk again about your feelings in the situation you just mentioned, but this time speak from a position of vulnerability.

_____

_____

What do you think your mate's reaction will be?

It is good to bring up those things your spouse is doing that aggravate your vulnerability. But communicate them from the point of view of your vulnerability—how what he does makes you feel—not as judgment against him. The first way engenders empathy, but the second just drives your mate away.

OBSERVE YOURSELF. Another thing that keeps mates from being known is that they speak, yell, fight, or react without first knowing what's really pushing their buttons. They do not monitor what they think or say; they just let their words fly without asking themselves what is really going on.

When, recently, have you had a reaction appropriate to your feelings but not appropriate to the reality of the moment? Be specific about both your feelings and the recent incident.

While your reaction might be appropriate to what you felt, it is misplaced. It is not appropriate to what was said or meant. Your reaction is appropriate for some injury that happened to you in another time and place, perhaps caused by your family of origin or some past relationships, but not for now. What might be the source of the reaction you just described?

Couples who do well together recognize misplaced feelings, suspend their reactions, and monitor themselves. They don't react with rage or move away, but they do acknowledge that what prompts their feelings is coming from somewhere else, and they communicate that to each other.

★ Whatever occurred in the past to spur that surge of feelings is in fact real, even if the reaction in the present was more than what was called for. So talk with each other about it. What are some statements you could make to communicate your awareness that your reaction in the present was a case of misplaced emotions?

These shared vulnerabilities help the couple move closer to each other. The sad thing is that many couples, like Sharon and Tony, genuinely care for each other, but they just can't get to the care because *what needs to be cared about is never expressed.* The hurt is not owned by the person feeling it; instead, it is expressed in hidden overreactions.

★ When you feel strong negative reactions to your lover, stop and count to twenty. Listen to your internal dialogues. Take a time-out. Doing so hooks different parts of the brain than those that are having those strong feelings. A moment of reflection helps you see your mate for who he really is and understand what he really meant to say. What will you do to help yourself remember this tip in the heat of the moment?

GET RID OF THE THINGS THAT GET IN THE WAY OF BEING KNOWN. You are human, so you have a tendency to hide what you are really thinking and feeling. Don't get defensive or feel bad about this tendency. Yes, it's a dumb thing to do, but we come by it honestly, as everyone since Adam and Eve has done it. We cover our vulnerable selves, so we will be loved and approved of, desired and wanted. The paradox is that the very act of covering up keeps that from happening. Our defenses that are supposed to protect us from alienation and rejection ensure those very things.

What are you covering—and what are you using as a cover? Are you, for instance, covering . . .
❏ feelings with smiles, or independence, or withdrawal?
❏ vulnerability with anger?
❏ fear with pride and control?
❏ shame with performance and seeking admiration?
❏ inferiority with looking for approval from others?
❏ pain by acting like you are OK when you are not?

If you want to be understood, stop acting in ways that cover up what you are really feeling. If you have any doubts about what those are, review this list of some common ones and check any of your favorite walls or shields.

❏ Silence ❏ Sarcasm
❏ Withdrawal ❏ Nitpicking
❏ Overactivity ❏ Blaming
❏ Anger ❏ Meanness
❏ Argumentativeness ❏ Bitterness
❏ Indirectness ❏ Jealousy

Now ask your mate to tell you the ways you hide your true feelings and the ways your defenses get in the way of being known.

_____

_____

Take a few minutes to prayerfully consider why you don't want to be known and why you have chosen certain defenses as protection.

_____

_____

_____

The Guiding Principle

When you want to be understood, let this question be your guide: "Is what I am doing—or about to say—getting me closer to being known or farther away?" The good purpose for communicating is to make yourself known. That builds love. But there are some bad purposes for communicating that you must forsake.

Which of the following bad purposes have informed some of your communication with your lover? The desire, conscious or otherwise, to . . .

❑ Make your mate feel bad, stupid, or guilty
❑ Off-load anger, tension, or stress
❑ Let him know how bad you hurt by hurting him
❑ Make yourself be seen as right
❑ Alienate her and make her feel alone
❑ Dominate or control your mate in order to feel in control
❑ Throw off responsibility to him in order to feel "free" from control
❑ Blame her so you won't feel bad or wrong
❑ Hide your real feelings, hurt, pain, or fear
❑ Hide your failures

★ We have never seen anyone drawn in to greater intimacy by any of these methods. So what will you do to avoid acting on these purposes?

_____

_____

_____

A Lifeline: AS YOU COMMUNICATE WITH YOUR SPOUSE, BEGIN WITH THE END IN MIND. WHEN YOU SPEAK OR ACT IN RESPONSE TO YOUR MATE, DO YOU WANT TO BE KNOWN AND UNDERSTOOD? BEING KNOWN AND UNDERSTOOD IS THE FOUNDATION OF CREATING LOVE, INTIMACY, AND CONNECTION.

There's More to Listening than Hearing

Sheila and Wade had spent the weekend together, but she did not feel what she wanted to feel with Wade, which was a sense of togetherness that time together should produce. Hope was fading into detachment and disconnection. She was slowly unplugging.

★ Did you relate more to Sheila or to Wade? Why?

_____

_____

Wade could repeat Sheila's words, but he had not listened to her. Thinking that you are listening just by hearing the words is another dumb attitude that can sink your love life.

★ In your own words, explain the difference between hearing and listening.

_____

_____

_____

When do you tend to hear but not listen?

_____

_____

_____

In this section, we'll show you how to listen and not just hear.

The Truth About Listening

Wade did not get the real meaning of what Sheila was saying. It was not a question of whether he intellectually understood the content of her words. That is only the beginning of listening. That is just receiving the information. Listening takes more than getting information.

Wade insisted, "I know that listening is more than just getting information. It's also really understanding what the person is saying. I really understood what Sheila was saying. She felt alone. I got it. I totally got it." Do you think Wade "got it"? Why or why not?

_____

_____

★ Listening is more than just getting the information and understanding it. Listening has occurred only when the other person *understands that you understand*. What do you do and/or say to communicate to someone—to your mate—so that she understands that you understand? If you're not sure you're very good at this, ask your mate—and finish reading this section!

_____

_____

_____

Like Wade, you need to communicate to your spouse clearly enough so that *she understands that you understand*. You need to communicate to the point that she really feels that you understand—not agree necessarily, but understand and care. Worry about fixing the situation later. At the moment, just make sure she understands that you understand.

Empathy Is the Key

The key to connecting with each other is empathy, *the ability to identify with someone else's experience, feelings, and thoughts.* The focus is on the other person and on communicating to the other person that you feel what she feels.

When has someone's (ideally, your mate's) empathy been a source of comfort and hope?

_____

_____

_____

When Wade communicated that Sheila's feeling of loneliness was horrible, that he never wanted her to feel that way, and that he wanted to do something about it, he showed empathy. He showed that he was sensitive to her pain and was able to experience what it was like to be her for a moment. At that point, she felt understood and connected.

To empathize with your partner is to validate her experience. That doesn't mean that you agree with it or that it is right. It just means that you see that her experience is real. You recognize the truth that she feels that way. You say, "I see. What I did made you feel really hurt." You validate that the hurt is real, that you experience it with her, and that you care. Does this sound like a difficult assignment? Why or why not?

_____

_____

_____

When Empathy Is Absent

The opposite of validation is *invalidation*, which means to discount, or treat as not real or not true, what the other person is thinking, feeling, or experiencing.

When, if at all, do you tend to do this? Why?

_____

_____

_____

Look again at the insights into a man's response to a woman expressing her feelings (Book pg. 157). Men, what insight into yourself did those few paragraphs give you?

_____

_____

_____

Women, what insight into your man did you gain from that brief discussion?

_____

_____

_____

Men—and some women—tend to want to solve the problem instead of just listening and understanding. If that's how you are, why do you think you're so anxious for your mate's feelings to go away?

_____

_____

_____

Learn to listen without defending yourself or devaluing your mate's experience. Failure to listen will keep you from getting the connection you want in your love life, and all the defensiveness in the world will only defend something not worth holding on to, whether it's pride, ego, independence, old patterns, or whatever.

Learn to Listen

Give up your defensiveness and pride, and learn to listen to your mate.

Review the tips listed below. (They're more fully defined on Book pgs. 156–158.)

- FOCUS. Look your partner in the eyes and give all of your attention.

- MONITOR YOUR THOUGHTS. As your partner speaks, are you listening or thinking of your response?

- RESPOND NONVERBALLY. Let her know you are with her and truly listening.

- WATCH YOUR DEFENSIVENESS. Do not defend yourself or counterattack.

- EMPATHIZE. Communicate back what you have heard.

- CHECK IT OUT. Ask your mate what you do that keeps her from feeling listened to.

- DON'T TRY TO FIX IT. Connect first just through hearing.

- DON'T MAKE IT ABOUT YOU. Listening is about the other person.

Which tip are you already doing well? (Your mate will be able to confirm your answer.)

_____

Which tip will you act on this week? (If there are too many to choose from, consider asking your mate for input.)

_____

Connection Equals Being Known

As we have said, reconnecting with each other involves your hearts being known. And there is no way to be known if you are not listening to each other.

> What message do these scripture verses have for you personally?
>
> "He who answers before listening, that is his folly and his shame" (Proverbs 18:13).
>
> _____
>
> _____
>
> "The purposes of a man's heart are deep waters, but a man of understanding draws them out" (Proverbs 20:5).
>
> _____
>
> _____

A Lifeline: THE MORE YOU LISTEN AND DRAW OUT THOSE DEEP WATERS FROM YOUR LOVER, THE MORE YOU WILL KNOW EACH OTHER AND REESTABLISH THE CONNECTION AND LOVE LIFE YOU DESIRE.

Common Communication Stoppers

When Wade described his response to Sheila, my heart sank. I (Henry) had now experienced firsthand his failure to listen to her, and I felt the same kind of despair that she felt when trying to communicate to him. In an instant, he said something that made connecting absolutely impossible. It's as if we were building a bridge, and right in the middle of the process he dynamited everything.

Before you look closely at what follows, think about your relationship. When you hear the phrase *shutdown*, what recent interactions and/or communication patterns come to mind?

_____

_____

When have you felt caught in a prison cell, trying to send a message through the bars to your mate but not having your message make it through? What did you do with that feeling?

_____

_____

Maybe you don't feel caught in a prison cell. Could your spouse feel that way? Explain why you answered yes or no.

_____

_____

While no one ever communicates perfectly, some people do it much worse than others. They perpetually say things that not only do not help but make things even worse. It's a dumb thing to do, of course, but many do it without realizing what they're doing, and certainly without realizing there is a better way. But there is.

★ What are some of your bad communication habits? (I know; it's easier to talk about your mate's bad communication habits!)

Find and Fix Your Communication Stoppers

You've seen some of the following items elsewhere in this book, but the list below is a guide for what *not* to do when trying to connect with your mate. Learn them well—and learn to catch yourself *before* you do them.

Here's your assignment. Find your behaviors in this list (discussed more completely on Book pgs. 159–165) and then *just stop doing them*! It's really that simple.

1. DON'T DEVALUE WHAT YOUR MATE SAYS. No matter what you think of it, when your mate says something, take it seriously. Treat your partner with respect. *Really listen;* don't just hear the words.

2. DON'T MINIMIZE IT. When your spouse feels something strongly or thinks something is significant, you have to connect with that feeling, not try to shut it down.

3. DON'T GET DEFENSIVE. LISTEN TO YOUR PARTNER, take in what he says, and embrace it. Doing so means that, because you love your mate, you are more willing to hear than to defend yourself.

4. DON'T CRITICIZE OR PUT DOWN YOUR MATE. Complaints voiced in a critical spirit do not solve problems like constructive feedback does. So say what must be said in a way that is not a put-down or character assassination.

5. DON'T OVERREACT OR ESCALATE. Learn your reaction patterns so you will know when the pressure gets to a

place where you are not responding but reacting and overreacting. When you feel yourself overreacting, take a time-out and calm down.

6. AVOID "SHUTDOWN" STATEMENTS AND BEHAVIORS. Shutdown statements are things that you say when you are mad, hurt, or overwhelmed that totally stop the communication.

7. DON'T SHIFT THE BLAME. Shifting the blame means explaining away responsibility for your own behavior as being caused by your mate's behavior. Responding to feedback with a counteraccusation always stops the connection.

8. AVOID SARCASM. Sarcasm communicates only disdain and lack of respect. Besides killing whatever message was intended, sarcasm hurts, closes down hearts, and turns things in the wrong direction.

9. AVOID EXTREMES AND GLOBAL STATEMENTS. Such statements ("always," "never," etc.) are neither true nor helpful. They just leave the other person judged and feeling bad.

10. DON'T IMMEDIATELY JUMP TO YOUR PERSPECTIVE. Certainly conversation is give and take, back and forth. But some people do not connect with the other person's experience. They take a comment as the signal to talk about their side of things only. The other person is just left hanging.

11. DON'T TRY TO FIX IT. Most of the time, a problem that involves feelings can't be fixed until the feelings are heard and understood. Other times, the problem doesn't need to be fixed, just heard and understood. Solving this problem is pretty simple. Just shut up and listen.

12. DON'T GO "ALL BAD." One of the most infuriating things that people do in communication is to play the "all-bad victim." That role negates your spouse's feelings, the focus shifts back to taking care of you, and she is lost.

★ So what did you see about yourself when you looked into the mirror this twelve-item list offers? If you're not sure, keep reading!

_____
_____
_____

Look at Your Communication Stoppers

We all have things that get in the way of communication. You can go a long way toward rescuing your love life if you find out what your personal communication stoppers are.

Ask each other and talk about the way it feels when you do those things. Do not defend why you do them. Just listen to how it makes your mate feel.

Enlist each other's help to watch for these communication stoppers. Make it a project. Make up a signal, if necessary, by which one can tell the other when it is happening.

Which of the twelve communication stoppers are you going to work on this week? What's your plan of attack? Be specific.

_____
_____
_____
_____
_____
_____
_____
_____
_____

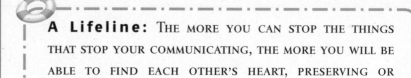

A Lifeline: THE MORE YOU CAN STOP THE THINGS THAT STOP YOUR COMMUNICATING, THE MORE YOU WILL BE ABLE TO FIND EACH OTHER'S HEART, PRESERVING OR REESTABLISHING THE CONNECTION.

Living What I Learn

Which of this section's five topics did you find most relevant or helpful? Explain.

- ❏ Don't Hide Your Feelings
- ❏ Choose to Face Reality
- ❏ Are You Saying What You Really Mean?
- ❏ There's More to Listening Than Hearing
- ❏ Common Communication Stoppers

_____

_____

_____

★ Share one or two insights from the text that you found especially encouraging.

_____

_____

_____

Which of the following lifelines will you grab this week? What specific step(s) will you take to help rescue yourself and thereby rescue your marriage?

- ❏ In good relationships, talking is honest and free of hedging, hiding feelings, and nuances. Work on talking like that!

- ❏ Love and reality can—and must—go together to preserve your connection, and acting on the eight tips for connecting first with grace can help.

❏ As you communicate with your spouse, begin with the end in mind: Speak or act in response to your mate in a way that makes you known and understood.

❏ Listen to and draw out those deep waters from your lover—and the more you will know each other and reestablish the connection and love life you desire.

❏ The more you can stop the things that stop your communicating, the more you will be able to find each other's heart, preserving or reestablishing the connection.

_____

_____

_____

As you close in prayer, ask God to help you look at yourself honestly so that you can see what you need to work on—and then ask Him to enable you to do that work.

When you go to the meeting, be ready to . . .
- SHARE YOUR ANSWERS TO THE STARRED (★) QUESTIONS.
- CHOOSE WHICH OF THE LIFELINES YOU'LL GRAB AND WORK ON THIS WEEK.

During the week . . .
- AS YOU WORK ON YOUR SECTION 5 LIFELINE, PAY ATTENTION TO THE EFFECTS OF YOUR EFFORTS ON YOU, ON YOUR MATE, AND ON YOUR MARRIAGE.

DUMB ATTITUDE #6

"My Lover and I Should Never Fight"

Conflict is normal in love. It is not a relationship-ender; it is part of love. In fact, *good conflict enhances a good love life.*

What did you learn about conflict when you were growing up? Be specific.

_____

_____

_____

Most of the time, conflict is not the problem. *The issue is the way that couples disagree and argue.* What insight into your connection does this statement give you? Explain.

_____

_____

_____

We are going to show you how to avoid the dumb ways to have conflicts—and how to have conflicts in a way that helps. After all, you will argue. You will disagree. You will have differences of opinion. If you don't, one of you is not necessary.

What new appreciation of conflict, if any, have you gained in only this brief introduction?

This section will also provide you with tips on how to use conflict to enhance love, intimacy, and passion. Are you skeptical? Already able to use conflict in such a way? Or something else? Explain.

Couples who know how to disagree in ways that redeem, heal, and connect find that they are closer and more loving. So don't be dumb and continue to avoid conflict. Learn instead how to rescue your love life through the right types of conflict.

Am I fighting for myself, or am I fighting for the relationship? Lord God, looking at our fights through that lens is helpful and convicting. Thanks for reminding me what's most important, whatever it is we're disagreeing about. Please teach us to fight in ways that redeem, heal, and build connection—and please help us love with Your love and forgive with Your grace. In Jesus's name. Amen.

Fighting for a Win-Win Solution

"We did it!" Kris exclaimed, and she and Bruce high-fived each other. They had had their first successful fight: they had argued over an issue, resolved it, and still felt connected to each other.

Bruce and Kris used to have very different kinds of fights. Kris felt alienated from Bruce because she couldn't bring up any problems to him without him becoming defensive and blasting her. On her end, Kris would disconnect from Bruce, leaving him feeling lost. In what ways are your fights with your lover like this earlier picture of Kris and Bruce? Be specific.

_____

_____

_____

In what ways are your fights with your lover like Kris and Bruce's "successful" fight? Again, be specific.

_____

_____

_____

Let your goal for fighting successfully with your lover be Kris and Bruce's goal: being able to argue and still stay attached.

Why Fight Anyway?

Couples who know how to fight right will love right. Healthy arguments are an important part of connection, reconnection, and passion. After all, at its healthy core, fighting is about love.

It is an attempt to resolve differences so that love can return or grow.

When people fight, they are defining themselves so that two distinct people can be close and yet keep their distinctness. A fight is a vigorous way to solve the problem of two people disagreeing while wanting to remain connected. Look back on a recent fight with your partner from this perspective. What distinctness was at stake? What evidence do you see that you and your lover wanted to remain connected?

_____

_____

_____

Fighting clarifies the definitions of the two people. He becomes aware that she is not an extension of himself and has her own thoughts and feelings—and vice versa. This awareness creates a space between the two lovers. That space is necessary to create passion, longing, and desire.

★ Remember the analogy of the test tube? What does that metaphor help you appreciate about the value of fighting?

_____

_____

What are most of your fights about—preferences (movies and restaurants), values (honesty and faithfulness), communication ("I never said I thought you looked fat in that dress"), or personal issues (baggage from the past)?

_____

_____

No matter what sparks the fight, you need a way to address these and any other disagreements you might have.

Keep the Goal in Mind

Couples who fight well keep the goal in mind: connection. Certainly you must focus on the problems themselves, but that is not the ultimate goal. *What is important is not the problem; it is how the problem affects the relationship.*

In what ways do you become a three-year-old in the heat of an argument?

_____

_____

_____

What might help you keep in mind that the argument is about relationship and having a better connection?

_____

_____

_____

Can your relationship handle one or both of you getting things off your chest? If so, what gloves do you and your lover wear when you do so? If not, what's a better way— a better time and place—for you two to talk about things that need to be talked about?

_____

_____

_____

_____

We all need a little catharsis now and then, but realize that this may work better in a subsequent conversation with your lover in order to keep the present fight from needing too much damage control.

Be Direct and Specific

Good fighters are direct and specific. When you are direct, you give your partner someone to talk to. And when you are specific, your partner knows exactly what you are seeing as the problem and, hopefully, what steps are required to change things.

What is your response when someone (including your mate) is direct and specific with you? Do you find it helpful? Does it put you on the defensive? Describe your reaction.

_____

_____

What is your spouse's reaction to someone being direct and specific?

_____

_____

If you don't know the answer to the preceding question, is it because you struggle to be direct and specific when you're fighting with your spouse? If so, what do you think that's all about?

_____

_____

_____

Was "direct and specific" communication modeled in your home growing up? If not, you may need a good example (Book pg. 170). Following that model, state a current concern in direct and specific terms.

Many fights center on vague charges, such as, "You do the wrong things and you don't do the right things." Where can you go with that? Be direct and specific.

Keep It Two-Way

Good fighting is much more than conveying your feelings and requests. It is a dialogue between two people. Don't get caught in the thinking that if you say your piece, it's all done. Most likely, your lover has his own realities and emotions about the situation, and he needs equal time. Only after he has his say can you solve the problem. If you fail to make it a conversation, things will only end up with alienation or escalation.

How often are fights with your spouse one-way conversations? Whether you do all the talking or don't get to talk at all, what is your contribution to the fact that the conversation is one-way?

★ What do you do—or could you do—to keep your fights a two-way conversation?

As a couple, learn to keep the conversation two-way. For starters, get used to saying, "When I am done I want to know what you think, because I want this to be about the two of us. And then we need to come up with a solution together."

Have a Structure

Ever notice how some of your fights are often the same fight over and over again? Each of you knows what the other will say.

What fight, if any, do you and your mate fight over and over again?

_____

_____

_____

What is the underlying issue?

_____

_____

_____

Fighting the same fight over and over is a signal that the issue has not been resolved. It needs to be resolved for good if possible, and that will require some structure.

Review the following possible structures. What does each phrase suggest?

• Traffic cop _____

• Time limits _____

• Agree beforehand on escalation _____

★ Which of these suggestions is most helpful for you? Why?

Now take a moment to consider anger, an emotion that is part of a relationship and part of disagreeing. Relationships have passion, and anger is part of passion. But pay attention to the degree and tone of anger.

Is the degree of the anger you tend to demonstrate appropriate to the situation? Or is it so great that it distances or scares your partner? You may need to talk to your partner to answer these questions!

Are you or your partner afraid of anger in general? If so, that's a personal problem that needs its own work. You may, for example, need to talk with someone wise about what anger symbolizes for you. Does someone's anger mean that his or her love for you is destroyed? That you will be injured? That you or the other person is bad? Talking about this can lead to real healing and change.

Now consider the tone of your anger. Again, is it appropriate to the matter at hand—or are you often sarcastic, vengeful, or "guiltifying"?

When the issue is dealt with, the anger it sparked should go away. If it does not, something else is going on inside the person that needs to be dealt with.

Normalize Fighting

Normalize your arguments by taking the fear and power out of them.

Couples who become anxious and avoidant about fighting either will not solve their problems or will have enormous blowups when they do argue. Which of these two possibilities do you tend toward?

It is not uncommon for couples in love to have some sort of disagreement every day, ranging from what time dinner was to how much someone spent. These disagreements don't have to be a big deal, but they will be if you try to avoid them. Is there potential for disagreement every day, but you're staying away from the issue? What's motivating that choice?

One way to normalize fighting is to, when you are *not* fighting, refer to your fights as a part of your life together: "Remember that trip we took to the river? It was the day after that fight we had about your mother's visit." What fights, if any, serve—or could serve—as markers in your history together?

Another way to normalize fighting is to, when you *are* fighting, talk about it in the "now": "Look, I know we're both mad right now, but I want you to know that I love you and I want us to be safe with each other." Will you be able to do this? Why or why not?

_____

_____

_____

Such efforts to normalize fighting help integrate love, truth, reality, and passion into the connection.

A Lifeline: ABOVE ALL, REMEMBER THAT FIGHTING IS NOT DONE FOR ITS OWN SAKE. FIGHTING IS FOR THE SAKE OF LOVE, RELATIONSHIP, AND CONNECTION. ANY ARGUMENT SHOULD BEND ITS KNEE TO LOVE.

The Fatal Flaw in Fairness

Life is not fair. Neither are relationships. Deal with it. The reality is basically this: *if you demand fairness, you stand to ruin your love life.*

What has been your take on the role or importance of fairness in relationships?

_____

_____

★ What, if anything, about the statements that open this chapter surprised you?

_____

_____

_____

Shouldn't we be fair with each other? Isn't that what give and take is about? If I don't require fair treatment, won't I receive bad treatment? To answer these concerns, let's look at what a demand for fair treatment really means and go from there.

What is fairness? In relationships, it means that each partner should receive to the degree that he gives to the connection. In a marriage relationship, the thinking would go something like this: _I have been kind and loving to my lover. He has not reciprocated. Therefore, I am justified in withdrawing my kindness and love from him, for I am not receiving fair treatment._

Fairness and Connections

The truth is, this principle works in business and tasks, but not in connections. Connections were never meant to be based on fairness.

What personal experience of yours supports that assertion?

_____

_____

_____

THE FOUNDATION OF INTIMACY IS ATTACHMENT, NOT PERFORMANCE. Relationships are established on closeness, vulnerability, and love. But when someone takes the stance that he will give no more than he receives, the entire foundation has been shifted to performance. Now he is in the relationship for what he can get, and he won't give until he gets that. Love has to take second place.

Explain in your own words the relationship between fairness and performance.

Remember the lover who felt neglected and, in turn, neglected his mate? That was technically fair, but what impact did his choice have on the connection?

What situation in your relationship, if any, did that example remind you of? More specifically, when have you done something less than helpful to the relationship in order to keep things between you and your spouse even and fair? What resulted?

Relationships based on performance and fairness can't work. There is not enough love and grace to hold things together. Watch how a five-year-old gets angry with her friends, then takes her ball and goes home. She has her ball, and she doesn't have her friends. But she feels that fairness has been accomplished.

It's far better to base the relationship on love and attachment rather than fairness. Forget fairness; opt for humility. When has—or when might have—humility served your connection well? Was it humility on your part or your lover's? Describe the situation.

What opportunity to choose humility over fairness do you currently have?

FAIRNESS IS ANTI-LOVE. Fairness is *giving to get*, a concept that has no place in love. Scorekeeping is just a way to make sure you'll get yours back, which reveals the intent that you were in it for yourself in the first place. Giving to get will never result in the love you need.

How would you feel if your partner said, "I'll spend time being close to you and connecting to you, if you'll pay me"? What point do this question and your answer drive home about fairness and love?

Couples who give more than they get tend to receive more too. The practices of grace, patience, and sacrifice are planted in each other's hearts and minds, and each knows that he or she is special and valuable to the other. And that, in turn, generates more love in a way that fairness never could.

FAIRNESS DISTORTS REALITY. Living by the fairness ledger also doesn't work because we have a tendency to distort the ledger the way a funhouse mirror distorts our reflection. Fairness distorts reality.

★ Why is it easy for us to see our partner's failings very clearly—and not so easy to see ours?

Why do our partner's feelings seem so huge and ours so inconsequential?

Even when we are on the fairness system, we inadvertently cheat and skew the results so that we come out looking good. Better by far to forget the whole fairness thing and move on to love.

GOD IS NOT "FAIR." God models His relationship with us based on grace, not fairness. In light of how we have treated ourselves, one another, our world, and God, why is it good news that God is not "fair"? (Of course He is ultimately fair and just, but He does not insist that we be perfect in order to receive His love.)

One of the most profound and comforting realities of life is that God "does not treat us as our sins deserve or repay us according to our iniquities" (Psalm 103:10). What do our sins deserve? What would be the fair response on God's part?

_____

_____

_____

Theologically, God accomplished ultimate fairness by Christ's death for us; the innocent was substituted for the guilty for mercy's sake. Our response is to love Him back. In the same way, when you let go of insisting that your lover play fair, you are extending that sort of mercy to her. And that will increase her capacity to love you.

How to Transcend Fairness

It's easy to be trapped in a five-year-old's "But that's not fair!" mentality. Here are some ways to grow beyond it and into true love and connection.

TALK ABOUT NEED INSTEAD. When you two have a conflict or a problem in the relationship, agree that instead of keeping score of who's being the better partner, you discuss need. Look again at the three examples (Book pg. 176).

For what current situation are you tempted to report a score rather than talk about need? Based on what these examples teach, word your concern in terms of your need.

_____

_____

_____

AGREE THAT YOU WILL GIVE TO GIVE, NOT GIVE TO GET. Get the issue out on the table, and admit that sometimes you are kind or attentive in hopes that the scorecard will qualify you for treatment in kind.

In what situations do you tend to act a certain way in order to be treated in that way? Why is the following statement a better, healthier approach? "I am going to love you because I love you, not so that you will love me. If you catch me keeping score, you have the right to bust me for it."

SOLVE PROBLEMS IN TERMS OF DISTANCE, HURT, AND RESPONSIBILITY, NOT FAIRNESS. Review the direct, accurate statements (Book pg. 177) that lend themselves to solutions for conflicts and keep you away from the scorecard.

For what current situation are you tempted to report a score rather than talk about the issue in terms of distance, hurt, and responsibility?

WHEN YOU RECEIVE MERCY, GIVE LOVE AND GRATITUDE. Realizing that your lover no longer has you on the ledger and is treating you with kindness simply because he loves you will help open your heart to him.

This week, work on extending that kind of mercy and love to your spouse. Note what happens in your relationship.

Being loved for ourselves—experiencing authentic love, with no strings attached, the way it was designed and intended by God—frees us, heals us, and brings us closer to our lover in a way that most of us can hardly imagine.

 A Lifeline: STORE THE FAIRNESS LEDGER SOMEWHERE ON THE SHELF SO YOU CAN TAKE IT DOWN SOMEDAY AND REMINISCE ABOUT IT JUST FOR GRINS.

Love Is Eternal When Forgiveness Never Ends

When I (John) ask most new couples, whether newly dating or newly wed, "How do you guys forgive when one of you hurts the other?" they're stumped. They look at me and cock their heads like my dogs do when they don't know what I am talking about (which is often).

★ Whether you are newly wed or long wed, answer the question "What does forgiveness look like in your relationship?"

> What did you learn about forgiveness when you were grow-
> ing up? Be specific about what you learned in church and
> what you learned in your family by words and/or actions.

Most people learned about forgiveness as part of religion, not
as part of relationships. So they don't really have a place for it
in their connection. But they must make a place for it, because
forgiveness establishes a principle that's key to keeping their
love life afloat: *your ability to connect and reconnect will
depend largely on your ability to forgive each other.* In other
words, good lovers are good forgivers, and vice versa.

The Debt

Simply put, forgiveness is when you *cancel a debt.* It's a legal
word. It first assumes that one person has hurt another, and
there is a debt to be paid. That is what the law is all about. A
crime must be punished in order to achieve justice and vindi-
cate innocent people. But forgiveness takes justice in another
direction. Though there is a justifiable debt to be paid, with
forgiveness the *penalty is cancelled.* There is no punishment.
The guilty go free.

> When have you experienced the freedom of forgiveness—
> the Lord's forgiveness or the forgiveness of another person?

When have you extended that kind of forgiveness to someone? Why did you do that?

_____

_____

_____

Strictly speaking, forgiveness flies in the face of justice. Guilty people should pay a fine, go to jail, or be punished in some way. But forgiveness transcends all that. It says, "Let him go." It gives a person another chance at life and growth. And nowhere is that more clearly illustrated than at the Cross.

Explain why forgiveness is the foundation of the Christian faith. Refer to Romans 3:23 and 1 John 4:10. This theology _is the only hope any connection has to grow and flourish in intimacy._

_____

_____

_____

There are only two ways to relate to each other: through the law and through forgiveness. No third alternative exists. Forgiveness is the only hope. When one partner incurs the debt, the other feels the pain and knows she has been wronged. _But she lets go of her right to demand justice._ She lets the prisoner go free, so to speak.

The Benefits

If we stopped here, we would not have made a strong case for a couple to learn forgiveness. It just doesn't seem right, fair, or healthy. But there are strong benefits in building this capacity into your love life. Let's take a look at them.

BOTH PARTNERS GET ANOTHER CHANCE. It's natural for us to want our partner to receive law and for us to receive forgiveness. But healthy couples realize that they both will fail each other and that both need to be forgiven—often.

Write out your own "golden rule" of forgiveness.

GRACE WINS. Forgiveness unlocks the grace you both need to keep the connection alive. Couples who forgive well know how deeply they both need the grace that comes from forgiveness, and because they receive it from each other, they are secure in the relationship.

Why is forgiveness one manifestation of grace? And why does forgiveness lead to security?

THE FORGIVER IS FREE. When you do not forgive, the hurt still owns you. When you cancel your partner's debt, you are free to move ahead and live your life. Forgiveness is a benefit to the wounded party.

When have you experienced this wonderful truth?

_____

_____

_____

What can you forgive your lover for so that you can experience this truth anew?

_____

_____

_____

FORGIVENESS BRINGS GRATITUDE. When you tell your partner, "I forgive you for what you did," you are lifting a burden of condemnation from him. In healthy people, this results in a deep and profound sense of gratitude.

What forgiveness from your spouse would prompt heart-felt gratitude from you?

_____

_____

_____

Have you asked for that forgiveness?

_____

_____

_____

YOU CAN BE REAL. Couples who forgive don't have to hide their faults from each other, fearing rejection. They are secure enough in the forgiveness to know that they will make it through. So they are real, authentic, and honest with each other.

In what ways aren't you comfortable being real with your spouse? (You may answer this in your head and heart rather than on paper.)

_____

_____

_____

Why would forgiveness free you to be more real?

_____

_____

_____

Blast Through the Obstacles

Forgiveness is always the right thing to do, but it's not often easy. It does get easier over time as the couple experiences the benefits, but you will need to blast through a couple of obstacles to get to the good stuff. Here they are.

EQUATING FORGIVENESS WITH RECONCILIATION. Forgiveness and reconciliation are not the same. Forgiveness is your obligation to cancel the debt, as your own debt has been cancelled by God (Ephesians 4:32). It takes only one person to forgive, but it takes two people to reconcile. If your partner is still being hurtful or is not showing necessary attitude changes, you aren't reconciled. Keep confronting and dealing with the problem today, but let go of the past debt.

What about the distinction between forgiveness and reconciliation is helpful to you personally? Be specific.

HOLDING ON TO UNFORGIVENESS TO MAINTAIN DISTANCE. There are ways to stay safe other than withholding forgiveness. Setting healthy boundaries and limits is one. This keeps you in control of your life, while not having to live in the misery of withheld forgiveness.

In what relationship are you holding on to unforgiveness in order to maintain distance? What would be a better way to protecting yourself? Be specific.

INCREASING DEFICITS IN GRACE. Sometimes a partner will try and try to forgive, but the debt keeps reemerging in the form of angry feelings, protesting the injustice, recurring thoughts, memories, or dreams. Sometimes this is due to a lack of sufficient grace resource inside the hurt partner. It takes a lot of love, comfort, and grace to let go of our resentment and anger over wrongs.

What relationships in your life are a source of grace— and love and comfort—for you?

If your list is short or nonexistent, what will you do to surround yourself with good, safe people?

Allow yourself to receive the grace you need to let go of the debt. Grace comes from the outside and transforms us so that we can forgive.

Become a Forgiving Couple

Here are some ways to add the awesome power of forgiveness to your love life.

AGREE ON THE REALITY. At some point you need, as a couple, to agree that you are both going to fail each other all through your relationship. Agreeing on the reality of failure sets the stage for the need of forgiveness.

Are you ready to agree on this reality? Why or why not?

Is your lover ready to agree on this reality? Why or why not?

TALK ABOUT WHAT YOU WANT AND NEED. People need different things from their partners regarding forgiveness. Talk to your lover to learn what needs to happen in your relationship so that you both can experience the benefits of forgiveness.

In what way would you like your mate to demonstrate forgiveness to you? Be specific about words, tone of voice, timing, and so on.

_____

_____

_____

PRACTICE RECEIVING AND GIVING FORGIVENESS. Swallow your pride. "Would you please forgive me for ..." and "I forgive you for ..." need to be part of your normal vocabulary.

Do you find it easy to use words and to face each other eye to eye when you extend forgiveness? When you receive forgiveness?

_____

_____

_____

If it's not easy, spend some time in prayer or with a therapist to determine what is going on.

_____

_____

_____

HAVE A "NO-WAITING" POLICY. When you have a problem, go to the other person as soon as it is realistic and get the forgiveness ball rolling. Always take the initiative, whether you are the hurter or the hurtee.

Why don't we naturally want to go first in forgiveness?

What fear and/or pride lies behind such hesitation?

GO ALL THE WAY. When you forgive, really forgive. Cancel the debt and let it go. Grieve it, feel your sadness, and say good-bye to the right to punish.

Which of these steps is toughest for you to take?

Why do you think that one is tough?

We're not saying that you should never bring up or talk about the issue requiring forgiveness. You may have to talk about someone's behavior or selfishness or irresponsibility if it is an ongoing problem. That is how problems are resolved. But talk about it as a problem to be addressed, not as a blame from the past.

What ongoing problem, if any, do you need to address with your mate?

_____

_____

_____

What words will you use? Be sure they are free of blame!

_____

_____

_____

 A Lifeline: MAKE FORGIVENESS A PART OF YOUR WORLD IN THE SAME WAY FISH EXPERIENCE WATER: WATER IS SO MUCH AROUND THEM THAT THEY DON'T EVEN KNOW THEY ARE WET. MAKE FORGIVENESS A LIFESTYLE FOR YOUR LOVE LIFE. FORGIVENESS WILL KEEP YOUR LOVE LIFE FROM SINKING.

Humility Is a Door, Not a Doormat

I (John) love how television sitcoms teach us about handling conflict. One person does something that upsets his partner. Then she does something to get him back. They blow up at each other, go to their friends, and say, "I don't know what I ever saw in him." Then, before thirty minutes are up, they manage to reconnect and become close again—until the next episode.

What are some of your favorite lessons on love or relationships that you see in television sitcoms?

These shows can be entertaining, but they often display a problem that many couples face: *a failure to understand the value of humility.*

What—or what kind of person—do you think of when you hear the word humility?

Does *humility* carry positive or negative feelings for you? Explain.

You can usually see pretty toxic levels of self-righteousness and pride infecting sitcom connections. In real life, however, when couples learn how much they receive when they exercise humility, things can transform quickly from alienation to intimacy.

The Misunderstood Trait

Humility doesn't get a good spin in our culture. But, properly understood, it really opens up things in a connection. Basically, humility is *the capacity to experience the reality of who you are.* A humble person is one who has no grandiose illusions of herself in either direction—good or bad, strong or weak.

★ What new understanding of humility or new appreciation for this virtue does this definition provide?

_____

_____

_____

In light of this definition, why is humility able to "open up things in a connection"?

_____

_____

_____

Humility affects several main areas of love relationships.

HUMILITY RECOGNIZES YOUR NEED FOR YOUR LOVER. When we toss aside our natural pride and self-sufficiency, underneath it is need for our lover. A humble partner says, "We aren't doing well right now. I don't feel close to you with this problem. But I know that I still need you and I need our relationship. So I want to work on this."

Why do you—if you do—struggle to acknowledge your need for your lover?

_____

_____

Why do you—if you do—struggle to let your lover know that you need her?

_____

_____

_____

HUMILITY IS THE KEY TO THE RESOLUTION OF NOT ONLY CONFLICTS IN LOVE, BUT ALSO THE LOVE RELATIONSHIP ITSELF, because love is about allowing the other person to be able to get inside you. But you still must be the guardian of your own heart, and protecting it is the right thing to do (Proverbs 4:23).

If you find it necessary to protect your heart in your connection, what rules or structure have you established?

_____

_____

_____

Ideally, you won't have to worry too much, if at all, about self-protection. In that case you can embrace the value of humility: it keeps you in touch with your need as a pathway back to love.

HUMILITY ACCEPTS YOUR INABILITY TO CHANGE OR CONTROL YOUR LOVER. Remember that humility is about admitting reality. And one of the toughest realities is that you really have no ability to change or control your lover.

★ What freedom to love comes with acknowledging this reality?

_____

_____

_____

What freedom to be loved does your lover experience when you acknowledge and live according to this reality?

_____

_____

_____

Couples who know the value of humility also know that they are only bound to each other by love, not by fear. You were designed to be a force for God, for love and for growth with your partner. So absolutely be an influence with him.

In what ways is that different from attempting to control your lover?

_____

_____

_____

Say what you want and need. Be an example. Be strong and direct. But _do not attempt to control_. Be as protective of your lover's freedom as you are of your own.

HUMILITY RECOGNIZES YOUR OWN IMPERFECTIONS. Humble people don't pretend to be someone they are not. They admit and confess their weaknesses and failures to their partner.

What weaknesses and failures are weeds you've brought to your relationship? List them.

Which of these weaknesses and failures—these things you don't like about yourself, *but which are nonetheless real*— are you able to own? One way we demonstrate ownership of our weaknesses is by admitting and confessing them to our partner. If you haven't done so, you need to.

If you hide your bad parts or pretend they are not there, *you are not present in the relationship.* Your body is there, but you are not in the room. Humility ensures that you both "show up."

HUMILITY ALLOWS YOU TO SHOW HURT WITH-OUT RETALIATING. Remember the conflict resolution played out in the sitcom? "When your lover bugs you, bug him back." The problem is, this approach doesn't bring resolution, love, and connection.

When we act in humility, we don't give back what we receive; we give back better than we receive (Romans 12:21). When, if ever, have you chosen this high road, which is actually the low road of humility? What were the results? In what ways did the connection benefit— or might it have benefited?

When you are hurt by your lover, it's never a good thing. The best response, however, is not to lash back or retaliate, but to show your hurt to your partner. Such humility paves the way to love. When, if ever, has someone come to you on this path of humility? What impact did that humility have on your feelings for him or her?

_____

_____

_____

When you choose the humble approach in discussing your hurt, your lover sees what he has done to someone he loves instead of having to defend himself and deflect your anger. His empathy, compassion, and remorse are activated. Do you find that worth the risk of the humble approach? Why or why not?

_____

_____

_____

Humility brings about the best results because it doesn't play the fairness card. It plays the love and reality cards, which trump everything else in making a connection and rescuing love.

How to Create Humility in Your Love Connection

Here are some ways to build good and healthy humility into your relationship so that you can keep your conflicts constructive.

AFFIRM THAT YOU DO NEED EACH OTHER, EVEN IN CONFLICT. Practice saying these words out loud: "I need you, and I love you. Even when we are fighting, the need doesn't go away. And I want to resolve our conflicts so that it's easier to be safe with my need for you."

Why are these good words to say to your lover?

_____

_____

_____

If your partner uses your humility against you and deliber-
ately hurts you with it, you must stop everything immediately and insist that the problem be addressed, possibly
by a competent therapist. Do not go further until this has
been dealt with directly. Empathy should rule.

_____

_____

_____

REVEAL YOUR FEARS TO EACH OTHER. Why have
you not been as humble as you needed to be? Why have you
been proud or self-sufficient? Have you been afraid of rejection, being put down, controlled, or disrespected?

Tell each other about these fears.

_____

_____

_____

When you share your fears, reassure each other that you
don't want to be the cause of those feelings. Give each
other grace and safety so that humility can emerge,
along with the real person.

_____

_____

_____

ADMIT YOUR FLAWS BEFORE YOUR PARTNER BRINGS
THEM UP. You can do that when you don't want it to get in
the way of the love, when you want the issue resolved, and
when the relationship is safe enough for you to do so.

Look again at the two examples of admitting your flaws
(Book pg. 189). Could you make that kind of statement?
Why or why not?

_____

_____

_____

Will you commit to taking the first step in a conflict?
Why or why not?

_____

_____

_____

Remember that humility is about embracing what is true and
real about you. If you have been together for any significant
amount of time, it is not likely that the admissions are any sur-
prise to your lover. Rather, you are bringing into the relationship
what you both know to be true, so that you can deal with it.

CELEBRATE HUMILITY AND CONFRONT PRIDE.
When one of you admits need, limitation, or faults, throw a
party. Humility should draw you closer together and into the
deeper aspects of each other's hearts and souls.

When will you admit a need, limitation, or fault and test
the truth of this claim for yourself?

_____

A Lifeline: MAKE HUMILITY THE EXPECTATION AND PRIDE THE ABERRATION IN YOUR LOVE RELATIONSHIP. HUMILITY MELTS THINGS DOWN INSIDE SO THAT LOVE CAN FLOW FREELY. YES, HUMILITY IS A HARD PILL TO SWALLOW IN THE SHORT TERM, BUT IT BRINGS UNBELIEVABLE RESULTS IN THE LONG TERM. LIVE IN REALITY, ADMIT REALITY, AND GET ON WITH THE BUSINESS OF TWO REAL PEOPLE LOVING EACH OTHER.

How to Underreact to Overreactions

One of you gets a little peeved about some ordinary matter and says something like, "It really bugs me that you don't listen to me." The other partner explodes with rage, hurt, or both, in a manner far more intense than the initial statement justifies. The first person tries to calm things down, but nothing works. The explosion goes on for a while. In time the dust settles, but neither of you knows where to go from there, so you just hope it doesn't happen again.

What do you know from your relationship about emotional explosions and dust needing to settle?

Which of you is more likely to explode? Explain.

These explosions—called *overreactions*—must be understood and resolved in order for you to achieve the lasting intimacy you want in your love life. Read on, and we'll help you understand overreaction and resolve it.

What an Overreaction Is and Isn't

When a person overreacts, she is experiencing an emotional response (hurt, fear, rage, and guilt, among others) that is greater than normal, given the circumstances.

Describe your most recent overreaction. If you're not sure which emotional response to life qualifies as an overreaction, ask your mate.

Explain why you labeled that incident an overreaction.

Understand that, in one sense, overreactions are not overreactions. In objective reality, the emotions exhibited are greater than the situation, but *for that person's inner world, the emotions are entirely consistent with that situation.* He is living or reliving something that is still present within his experience. This has to do with hurt or pain that has not been dealt with, processed, or healed.

The normal process of resolving this sort of pain is through love, support, grief, forgiveness, and healing. Where do—or could—you go to receive these things? With whom are you safe and able to express the pain, work through it, and let go in the grief process? Or what will be your first step in a search for this kind of safe environment?

_____

_____

_____

Over time, and with the right steps, most hurtful events can be transformed into normal memories that instruct, teach, and warn us about life. But when this healing process does not occur, these *unprocessed memories are still experienced as occurring in the here and now.*

At this point, do you have any idea what the specific underlying cause of your overreactions might be? What mild or severe hurts have not yet been healed?

_____

_____

What insight do these statements offer you? What hope?

_____

_____

_____

What Triggers Overreactions

Whatever the cause of your overreactions, the triggering event is somehow similar to or represents a bad or dangerous event or relationship, and you react to it as a little child would. In your experience, you are back there when the bad thing happened to you.

Look at the list of sample triggers (Book pgs. 191-192). Do you recognize yourself in any of these situations?

_____

_____

_____

As in Randy and Melissa's case, overreactivity caused by past and unhealed wounds finally helped to bring them together and enabled them to connect in deeper and more satisfying ways. Be encouraged!

How to Help the Person Overreacting

Here are some solutions to this issue of overreactivity.

DON'T ATTACK THE IRRATIONALITY. You can't talk a person out of her feelings. So stop the argument and become safe. Exercise a little warmth and tenderness. Speak softly and empathize with her hurt, anger, and fear.

What will that warmth and tenderness look like? What will you say to empathize with her hurt, anger, and fear?

_____

_____

If you tend to overreact, answer these variations of the questions. What would you like your mate's warmth and tenderness to be like? What would you like to hear that would show her empathy with your hurt, anger, and fear?

_____

_____

_____

DON'T TAKE THE NEGATIVE EMOTIONS AS A PERSONAL ATTACK. When your partner overreacts, remember that you merely served as a trigger or symbol for the sins of someone else against her. Treat her as caringly as you would a small child who is having an emotional storm, and stay present, real, and containing with her.

PUT YOURSELF IN HER POSITION. Think of times you have been totally panicked or hurt, and how out of control and frightened you have felt.

What did you need at those times? Give those things to your spouse.

_____

_____

_____

When you've been totally panicked or hurt, you needed space, care, and time to calm down. Remembering this will help you have empathy, patience, and compassion for your lover's discomfort.

PROVIDE STRUCTURE AND REALITY IF NEEDED. Let your partner know that you aren't mad, that he is not in trouble with you, and that you will get through it.

Put these thoughts into words that you are comfortable saying. Practice right now.

_____

_____

_____

Also practice what will you say, for instance, to communicate, "I will be here and I will help you." Let him know that if the overreactions get too bad, you will get help. In most cases, the storms will subside with enough empathy, space, and time.

_____

_____

_____

Again, think of how a small child's reactivity gradually resolves as you hold him and keep him safe.

TALK ABOUT WHAT IT WAS LIKE FOR HIM. Your partner needs to discuss his overreactions during normal times, so that he feels connected to you.

Have you been avoiding (or tempted to avoid) discussing the problem of overreactivity? Why or why not?

_____

_____

_____

Plan such a time and then ask him what might help the next time he overreacts. Work together to develop an approach consisting of things you can do to help create an environment of comfort and safety. This routine will help him to stabilize that hurt part inside by increasing his internal sense of security and control.

```
_____
_____
_____
```

ROLE-PLAY AND PRACTICE SAFE CONFRONTATIONS.
Practice how to have disagreements that avoid the triggers.
Write your own script—or at least the opening scene—and
then be willing to ad lib.

What will you do to help your partner become aware of
what triggers your overreactions so that you both can
know what might be coming?

```
_____
_____
_____
```

★ What will you do to develop the ability for both of you to
give and receive feedback in loving and constructive ways?

```
_____
_____
_____
```

GET HELP IF NEEDED. If your partner's condition does
not resolve itself in a reasonable amount of time, seek help.
Many therapists are well-trained in helping people work through
their overreactions, and the results can be quite positive.

Where will you go to find names and, ideally, references?

```
_____
_____
```

A Lifeline: ULTIMATELY, THE HURT THAT CAUSES YOU OR YOUR LOVER TO HAVE THESE INTENSE EMOTIONS CAN BE TRANSFORMED AND MATURED. OVERREACTIVITY CAN GIVE WAY TO RESPONDING APPROPRIATELY, IN BOTH EMOTIONAL AND INTELLECTUAL WAYS, AND YOU CAN MOVE ON AS A COUPLE WITHOUT THE WILD EXPLOSIONS SINKING YOUR LOVE LIFE. BE A PART OF YOUR LOVER'S GROWTH, AND IN SO DOING, HELP THE RELATIONSHIP GROW IN LOVE.

Living What I Learn

Which of this session's five topics did you find most relevant or helpful? Explain.

❑ Fighting for a Win-Win Solution
❑ The Fatal Flaw in Fairness
❑ Love Is Eternal When Forgiveness Never Ends
❑ Humility Is a Door, Not a Doormat
❑ How to Underreact to Overreactions

_____

_____

_____

★ Share one or two insights from the text that you found especially encouraging.

_____

_____

_____

Which of the following lifelines will you grab this week? What specific step(s) will you take to help rescue yourself and thereby rescue your marriage?

❑ Remember that fighting is not done for its own sake. It is for the sake of love, relationship, and connection. Any argument should bend its knee to love.

❏ Store the fairness ledger somewhere on the shelf.

❏ Make forgiveness a part of your world in the same way a fish experiences water. Make forgiveness a lifestyle for your love life.

❏ Make humility the expectation and pride the aberration in your love relationship. Live in reality, admit reality, and get on with the business of two real people loving each other.

❏ Overreactivity can give way to responding inappropriately, in emotional and intellectual ways. When you respond appropriately, you are being a part of your lover's growth and helping the relationship grow in love.

_____

_____

_____

As you close in prayer, ask the Lord to help you do just that by the power of His grace and with His love. His grace can enable you to keep love more important than winning an argument, to forgive your spouse, to live in humility, to be an agent for change in your relationship, and to learn to respond rather than overreact.

When you go to the meeting, be ready to . . .
- SHARE YOUR ANSWERS TO THE STARRED (★) QUESTIONS.
- CHOOSE WHICH OF THE LIFELINES YOU'LL GRAB AND WORK ON THIS WEEK.

During the week . . .
- AS YOU WORK ON YOUR SECTION 6 LIFELINE, PAY ATTENTION TO THE EFFECTS OF YOUR EFFORTS ON YOU, ON YOUR MATE, AND ON YOUR MARRIAGE.

DUMB ATTITUDE #7

"My Lover Should Trust Me Without Question"

The reality is that you can love someone and not trust that person *at the same moment in time*. Though love and trust are often confused, they are very different parts of a relationship. Love is a gift that you give your lover, even when he doesn't deserve it. He must be proven worthy of your trust before you will provide it. Love is free. Trust is earned.

What do you find helpful about these definitions of *love* and *trust*?

What negative effect could confusing love and trust have on a relationship? Keep in mind that love is free and trust is earned.

Do you trust your mate? Rate your level of trust on a scale from one to ten. Let "ten" stand for "Absolutely" and "one" for "Not as far as I can throw him/her."

Explain why your mate earned that ranking—and the goal is not to bring out all the dirty laundry. If the list of reasons for a low score gets too long, you need to realize something about yourself and about your role in this aspect of your relationship!

Often, trust must be built—or rebuilt—for intimacy and rescue to happen. In this section, you will learn what trust is, how powerful it is, and what you can do to create a relationship based on both love *and* trust.

Lord God, You know how hard it is for me to trust my spouse. You know the circumstances, You know the pain, and You know the person involved even better than I do. I ask, Lord, for the ability to forgive my mate for the hurt that comes with broken trust, and I ask You to heal that hurt. I also ask, Lord, for wisdom as I learn how—and when and perhaps even if—to trust again. Please give me the courage to not be a doormat . . . and the grace and openness to learn to trust again. In Jesus's name. Amen.

Trust Is a Risk You Have to Take

Karen took a huge risk when she told Jim about her abortion. She didn't know if she could trust him with that part of her. What if he hated her or left? Despite those very real possibilities, she risked trusting Jim.

Comment on Jim's reaction to what Karen shared. Why is grace an appropriate word for his response?

_____

_____

_____

When, if ever, have you risked trusting someone, received grace, and therefore learned that the person was indeed worth trusting?

_____

_____

_____

Karen had my (John's) perspective and support: I felt that Jim could handle her confession, and I could pray for her. Who in your life can and will support you if you need to take the risk to trust someone?

_____

_____

_____

Trust is *the ability to be totally real, authentic, and unguarded with your lover.* It means being able to bring all parts of yourself to him, good and bad, strong and weak, without fear of condemnation or judgment. It has to do with not needing to edit or color what you say or who you are for fear of his reaction.

To what degree are you able to live out that kind of trust in your love relationship? Put differently, what parts of yourself—if any—are you unable to bring before your mate? And when—if ever—do you feel the need to edit what you say or do?

_____

_____

_____

In the Hebrew Scriptures, there is a word for trust (*batach*) that actually conveys the idea of "carelessness" (Psalm 22:9). When you trust someone, you aren't hypervigilant and paranoid about what you say or do. You let things slip sometimes, and even if that causes a problem, it's a little problem, not a catastrophe.

Think about the last time you opened up to your partner about a failure or a fear. When you were vulnerable with him, did he move toward you, make it safe for you, and draw you out? Or did he move away, become critical, or even dismiss the issue?

_____

_____

_____

This exercise is not meant to be an indictment of partners. It is simply a way for you, as a couple, to begin to evaluate the level of trust the two of you have in each other.

When your partner opened up to you about a fear or failure, what was your reaction? What did you do to make it
safe, to draw her out? Or did you become critical and
shut her down?

Couples who have learned how to trust receive many benefits
in return. They are able to connect at deeper levels. They desire
to be with each other and want to give to each other in gratitude. They are able to have more passion, as passion can
emerge only in a safe and trusting context. Trust forms the
foundation of the love life you want to have.

The Three Elements of Trust

Couples can work on trust and improve it. Let's look at three
primary elements that, when present in the relationship, create
an atmosphere of trust and safety.

RISK. No risk, no trust. To develop trust, you will need
to extend yourselves out of your comfort zone and take a risk.
Risk in a relationship involves exposing vulnerable parts of
yourself to your partner.

You will need to let him know about your thoughts, feelings,
and experiences that are negative, painful, or fragile.
This might include fears, hurts, mistakes, sins, and parts
of yourself that you are ashamed of or wish you didn't
have. What are some specific things you have not yet
risked sharing? Make a mental list, if not a written one.

Before taking the risk of sharing anything on your list, deal with any internal conflict. How do you think your lover will respond? And what would you like to be able to do and say in return?

Whatever your partner's response might be, you need to take the risk because *you are designed to bring every part of your being into the relationship*. God made you to connect at all levels.

Look again at the list (Book pg. 200) of things lovers some-times need to say that involve risk. Which one, if any, are you due to say? If none of those apply, think about the personal list you just made. Which one is a good-sized risk to take right now?

Couples who refuse to risk because they are afraid of the consequences may think they are protecting the relationship, but they are actually doing a dumb thing that will sink it.

WELCOME. Appreciate the effort and humility of your partner, who is doing something uncomfortable for the sake of the relationship. Extend grace and love with no hint of condemnation. You do not have to agree with what your partner says or does to be welcoming. The best way to understand it is that *you are welcoming your partner's vulnerability*, not necessarily the right or wrong of what he is saying.

★ Think "golden rule." Consider how hard it is for you to take a risk with him, and give him the same grace you would need. What words, emotional presence, and body language would you like to be welcomed with when you risk sharing a secret, a weakness, or a sin?

_____

_____

_____

★ What will you do to extend that same kind of welcome to your mate? Be specific about the words, emotional presence, and body language you will offer.

_____

_____

_____

As the two of you welcome each other's risks, you will grow able to believe, on a heart level as well as a head level, that your willingness to reveal your darker parts is truly welcome in the relationship.

TRUSTWORTHINESS. Trustworthiness has to do with the character of the two of you as individuals. Not only are you to risk and welcome, but you also need to earn each other's trust by how you handle these more fragile things. This requires time.

★ Trustworthiness means you are taking your partner's investment in you seriously and you will not do anything to break the trust between you. What can you do today or this week to show your mate you are trustworthy?

_____

_____

A couple who is trustworthy puts a high value on faithfulness, loyalty, and reliability. Which of these traits has been hardest for you to live out? Take a risk and talk to your mate about that fact. You might even ask for forgiveness, prayer support, and help.

_____

_____

_____

How Much Trust Is Too Much?

Ideally, you cannot trust too much. A love relationship was meant to give light and grace to all parts of you, so that you can safely know and be known and grow from that. In reality, however, you will need to find out what is possible at this point in your relationship and move on from there.

While figuring out where you two are on the spectrum of trustworthiness, the best rule of thumb is to risk at a level somewhere beyond comfort but not to the point of injury. So answer these questions: Are you feeling fragile right now? Does your relationship seem fragile? Does it have a history of untrustworthiness? If you answer yes to any of these three questions, start with a little risk before you take a big one.

_____

_____

_____

Couples working on trust are often concerned about confessions of indiscretion. They wonder, *Should I tell her about the lust or the affair?* This question is not simple to answer, and it must be determined on an individual basis.

What was your reaction to the guidelines (Book pgs. 202-203)?

What actions are those guidelines prompting you to take?

Obviously, this decision requires safe and mature counsel from others as well as much prayer for wisdom and sensitivity.

Building a Legacy of Trust

A man talking to Frank asked the inappropriate question "What about when you were overseas on military duty? I bet you've got a few stories Ruthie's never heard!" Frank's matter-of-fact response was, "I don't have any secrets from Ruthie."

Why is it a gift to have a lover who keeps no secrets from you?

What, if anything, is keeping you from giving that gift to your lover?

Trust is not a mystery. It's not an "either you have it or you don't" kind of thing. Trust can be developed and matured, and it's well within your power to do it.

> **A Lifeline:** WITHOUT RISK, YOU WILL NEVER KNOW IF YOU CAN TRUST YOUR LOVER. WITHOUT WELCOME, YOU WILL SIMPLY DETACH OR PRETEND. WITHOUT TRUSTWORTHINESS, YOU WILL NOT BELIEVE THE WELCOME IS REAL. MAKE ALL THREE A COVENANT IN YOUR CONNECTION WITH EACH OTHER.

Broken Trust Can Be Repaired

For a long time, Carl was not the most trustworthy of people. Though he cared deeply for others, he had difficulty being honest and reliable. His deceptive lifestyle cost him his career, and his marriage was not far behind. So Carl got help, and things began to gradually change. He began to be more truthful, more responsible, and more dependable with Susan and her feelings.

★ Rebuilding broken trust is never an overnight success. Why is that the case?

_____

_____

_____

What experience, if any, do you have with needing to rebuild broken trust? With needing to allow someone to rebuild your trust in him/her?

_____

What repair work, if any, does the trust level in your marriage need right now?

Again, rebuilding broken trust is never an overnight success. But Carl hung in there, and Susan did her part. In time, they began to rebuild the trust between them. Their journey illustrates the point that, when trust is broken, *there are ways to repair and rebuild it.* These ways involve work, humility, courage, and patience; but the process works as long as both parties engage in it.

Trust Problems Are a Serious Matter

Trust issues are in a relational category all their own because trust underlies and supports the entire fabric of the connection itself. When trust is broken, it's as if the foundation of one's home is cracked, and the home is no longer a safe place to live. When trust decreases, love decreases, and vice versa.

Is the foundation of your relationship at risk? Check if any of these trust-breakers exist:

❑ Deceit
❑ Manipulation
❑ White lies
❑ Financial indiscretions
❑ Sexual unfaithfulness at any level
❑ Minimizing the hurt you have caused your partner

❑ Saying one thing and doing another
❑ Broken promises and commitments
❑ Inconsistency as a person

Which of these trust-breaking behaviors, if any, do you need to stop doing? Let this exercise be a warning! What will you do to stop? Where will you go to find help and support?

_____

_____

_____

When you cannot trust someone, *you no longer know who he is.* Furthermore, if you have trusted your lover, you have exposed some vulnerable parts of yourself to him—weak, shameful, fearful, or bad aspects that can be fragile and easily wounded. Trust problems are matters of having the most fragile parts of the heart that you entrusted to your lover injured by him. Therefore, trust issues must be taken seriously. Rebuilding trust is work, but it's dumb not to tackle it. The work is definitely worth it. Let's go into what you can do to correct problems in trust.

Six Steps to Repair the Breach

If you have a trust problem, think of it as a crack in the foundation of your connection. How do you, as a couple who wants to rescue your love life, repair the breach? Here are the basic steps.

AGREE WITH REALITY. State and discuss what really did happen, and bring it into the light of your relationship. That is, talk about it frankly, while at the same time reaffirming the love and safety you have for each other. You simply cannot proceed unless both of you agree on the basic realities of what happened.

If you need to take the risk, do so with prayer and without defensiveness. Practice what you will say beforehand.

★ If you need to welcome your partner's risk of confession, plan ahead what you will do through your words, emotional presence, and body language to give your partner the grace you would want to receive.

TREAT IT AS SERIOUS. The likelihood for healing is much greater when the couple recognizes the seriousness of the problem. You may have to face some painful realities between the two of you in order to know what can be done. But it is paramount for both of you to be truthful and honest about not only what happened, but also its effects.

What effects of the breach in trust need to be addressed in your relationship?

❑ Your heart is broken.
❑ Your partner has hurt you deeply.
❑ You are unable to feel close to your partner.
❑ You don't know if you will ever be able to feel close again.
❑ You don't know if you are still in love with him.

★ What will you do to prepare to take this risk? Or what will you do to welcome your spouse as he takes this risk?

YOU CANNOT HEAL THAT WHICH IS NOT BROUGHT INTO THE RELATIONSHIP. Read that sentence again, and let that truth reinforce your commitment to do this important but crucial work.

Also, if you have broken trust, be sure to reread the paragraphs on Book pgs. 207-208: "It is extremely important—even critically important—for the partner who broke trust to listen closely to his mate's hurt. . . ." And "Never dismiss or minimize how your partner is feeling about your betrayal's effect on her. . . ."

DEMONSTRATE REMORSE AND REPENTANCE. The partner who violates his lover's trust needs to express and demonstrate authentic remorse and contrition. If you love someone, you aren't merely sorry you got caught. You feel bad for the hurt you caused. Let the one you love know how deeply you regret what you did.

If you have broken trust, practice expressing your remorse—and be sure that your words clearly communicate your sorrow for putting him through so much pain. It's not about you; it's about your partner.

_____

_____

Your remorse must be backed by *repentance*. To repent is to turn from our erroneous ways (Luke 17:3). It means action. What action does your indiscretion call for? Be specific and follow through; do what you say you will do. (See Book pg. 208 for a list of ideas.)

_____

_____

The injured person also has a task. You must hold to requirements and standards about these matters of change. Insist on them, talk about them, and don't waver. This is a burden you must carry, but you don't have to carry it alone. Whom will you ask to stand with you to help you keep the requirements intact?

_____

_____

_____

All too often the hurt person gives in to his love and loneliness and accepts "I won't do it again" as enough. That may be OK for a single, minor incident. But for repeated and severe patterns, you must stand firm.

GIVE THE PROCESS TIME. Time alone never healed a trust issue, just as putting the ingredients into a bowl will not produce a cake. But time is necessary as you both work together on renewing trust.

If you have broken trust with your lover, get into the process of growth rather than just trying harder or starting over afresh as if nothing has happened. What might that look like? You could, for example, talk to some wise person about why you chose to be untrustworthy. Was it the easy route? Were you angry? Did you want to protect a secret life? Ask God for illumination here. Also, what monitor power will you give your partner and other trusted people so that they, not just you, will decide when you have truly changed from the inside out? Be specific as you answer both these questions—and then get to work.

_____

_____

_____

_____

If you have been betrayed, you need to take responsibility for learning to forgive, to cancel the debt. You will need to let go of the demand to punish and vent wrath on your partner. That will involve growth, grieving, and loving support from God and others. Who will support your growth and grieving?

If you have been betrayed, you will also need to observe the changes your partner is making over time—for at some point, you will need to take another risk with him. When you are ready, when the healing is happening inside you, and when he has been proving himself a changed person, it will be time to dip your toe into the water and let him back into your heart. It is probably best to do this under the counsel of some wise people who are *for* both of you as well as the relationship. Who are those people in your life?

DEAL WITH BAGGAGE. Sometimes when trust has been broken, the problem is compounded because the hurt person has had to deal with trust issues from previous relationships. That kind of baggage makes the woundedness even greater.

If you are the wounded person, are you taking on a victim mentality? Be honest about whether you are feeling totally without fault and that all problems are his fault. A trusted friend can help you see if you are playing the role of victim, a role that will significantly slow down healing and reconciliation.

If you realize that you have brought your own trust issues into the relationship, where will you go to get help resolving them? You may need to find a good growth group, pastor, or counselor to help you confess the wound, receive grace and healing, and learn to trust again. You need to free your relationship from the past so that you will be able to work with your genuinely remorseful and repentant partner.

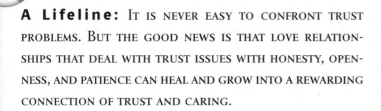

A Lifeline: IT IS NEVER EASY TO CONFRONT TRUST PROBLEMS. BUT THE GOOD NEWS IS THAT LOVE RELATIONSHIPS THAT DEAL WITH TRUST ISSUES WITH HONESTY, OPENNESS, AND PATIENCE CAN HEAL AND GROW INTO A REWARDING CONNECTION OF TRUST AND CARING.

Trust Thrives on Independence

When I was in college, my friend Mike explained to me (John) how my breakup with Cindy, my girlfriend, was my fault and not hers. Mike agreed that I had done a lot for Cindy—I had helped her with homework, walked her home, and done odd jobs on her apartment.

"Yes, you did all those things," Mike said. "And that's not all. You pouted when she had other things to do, gave her a hard time when she wanted to be with other people, and didn't like going out in groups with her. I think you suffocated her."

As I thought about Mike's analysis, I realized that I had pretty much smothered Cindy. At the time, I had thought my actions and attitudes were what people do and feel when they are in love. But in reality, it was more about me than about her.

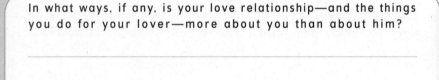

In what ways, if any, is your love relationship—and the things you do for your lover—more about you than about him?

_____

_____

_____

In what ways, if any, are the ways that you are "loving" your mate actually denying him healthy freedom and independence?

_____

_____

_____

The autopsy of my relationship with Cindy points out a key element in rescuing a love life: *you both need to encourage and develop independence and freedom within a context of love and connection.* This relates to the issues of dependency we covered previously, but here we deal less with personal dependency issues and more with establishing a strong relationship based on two people supporting each other's freedom and choices.

I and We

It takes two "I"s to form a "we." The "I"s don't disappear or melt into the "we"; they still exist. But something new has been added, which is the connection itself.

Your love connection is intended to keep a focus on both the needs of the individuals and the needs of the relationship. This focus must shift and change at times as seasons and needs change. When have you seen this shifting in your relationship? Give a specific example or two.

_____

_____

_____

Whenever the focus shifts, both of you must approve and support these two elements: the needs and interests of the individuals as well as those of the relationship.

THE "WE." There is built-in tension and sacrifice in being part of a "we." While you want to love and connect, you will probably resist giving up personal things in order to get that connection. After all, it's easy to think in terms of your own perspectives and interests, but it takes effort to think of what is best for your lover and the relationship.

What examples from your early days of marriage support the fact that "it takes effort to think of what is best for your lover and the relationship"? Perhaps you have a story about learning to give up total freedom, convenience, instant gratification, or having your way.

_____

_____

When has the importance of the "we" involved a significant sacrifice in your life together? Did your wife temporarily put off her career for the sake of raising children? Did your husband give up a promotion and transfer to another city to keep the family where they were doing well?

Choices for the "we" aren't easy, but they need to be faced from the perspective of what is best for the entire team.

THE "I." In the other direction, simply paying exclusive attention to the "we," is not good for the relationship either. Each individual's choices, preferences, needs, dreams, and desires are important.

★ When in your relationship have you seen that supporting the "I" brings many benefits to the "we"? Be specific.

What interests, hobbies, and friendships do you encourage— or could you encourage—your mate to be involved in?

Supporting your efforts to fulfill a goal can give your mate much happiness, knowing that your desire is being fulfilled. Then your own gratitude for her support can urge you to help her fulfill her own dreams as well.

Yes and No

Another important aspect of keeping your love life in balance is making the relationship a safe place to say no. Love grows when both partners are free to make choices. And it can't exist when that sort of freedom is resisted.

Consider the dynamics of your relationship. Who is the more assertive? Who is the more compliant?

When have you recently needed to say no? Comment on how easy it was for you and how well your mate responded.

When has your spouse recently needed to say no? Comment on how easy it was for her to say no and how well you responded.

Your relationship needs to place a high value on personal freedom. Otherwise, neither of you ends up getting what you want. If you want closeness and passion, let your lover have choices. If you want distance and coldness, try to control your mate. Which is the dumb attitude?

★ What can you, as a couple, do to turn the word *no* into a positive? Be creative!

Couples who have the freedom to move apart in their own choices and minds have more of a chance to connect and engage. Couples who don't have that freedom may look like they're close, but in time that closeness generally shows its true colors as an external compliance that often results in a cold heart and a dead connection.

If one or both of you has trouble hearing the word *no*, it may be helpful to look at the situation in three ways. First, don't you want your own choices also? What you want for yourself, you must also provide for the other. Second, if your lover stays around only because she's afraid to say no, you don't have her anyway. And third, your resistance to independence is probably a problem in other areas of your life, like work, friends, and family. What have these three questions helped you better understand about the value of the word *no*?

_____

_____

_____

Learning to accept *no* will help you not just in your love connection, but also in your success and happiness as a person.

Declare Your Independence

Pay attention to the choices and independence each of you has in the connection. The less control you have, the more connection, desire, and love will develop. Here are some tips for declaring your independence in the relationship.

HAVE A "FREEDOM OF CHOICE" TALK. Talk about the fact that freedom and love go together. Express your love, and reassure each other that you are committed to the relationship.

Do both of you understand that freedom and love go together? Explain why you answered yes or no.

When reassurance of your mutual commitment to the connection is firmly established, you can talk about how you want more choices and independence within the parameters of your connection. What specific choices and new independence would you like to enjoy? Thinking ahead will help you be prepared to talk with your mate.

ESTABLISH A VISION FOR INDEPENDENCE. Discuss the advantages of independence. For instance, free choices means that when you are there for each other, you are there wholeheartedly and by choice, not out of guilt.

★ What do you and your lover see as some of the advantages of independence?

Clarify either in your own mind—or in a discussion with your mate—the fact that independence does not mean selfishness or irresponsibility. In other words, define *independence* as you imagine it being lived out in your relationship.

Immature people want more freedom simply because they don't like the normal constraints of relationship, but commitment brings with it certain constraints. You cannot, nor should you, have all the same freedoms in a committed relationship that you had in your totally single life. In healthy connections, both mates give up certain freedoms because the advantages transcend what they had to surrender.

ESTABLISH AN ONGOING SYSTEM TO MONITOR FREEDOM. Agree that if one of you feels controlled, smothered, or guiltified by the other, it's OK to say so. Often the freedom resister is unaware that he is doing this, and he may need a little feedback, reminding, and coaching.

When your lover makes a freedom decision, how do you want to respond? Be specific about your words, tone of voice, and body language.

_____

_____

_____

When your lover balks at one of your freedom decisions, how do you want to respond? Again, be specific about your words, tone of voice, and body language.

_____

_____

_____

PAY ATTENTION TO THE BENEFITS. As you take the risk of being independent within your connection, become aware of what you should be getting in return.

When, if ever, have you had a taste of independence and found yourself missing your lover and looking forward to being with him?

Why does it make sense that freedom to make choices would create in your heart an expanding space that creates more room for love of your mate?

A Lifeline: ALLOW AND EXERCISE RESPONSIBLE FREE-DOM IN YOUR RELATIONSHIP, AND YOU SHOULD BEGIN TO NOTICE AN INCREASE IN THE THINGS BOTH OF YOU REALLY WANT IN YOUR LOVE LIFE: PASSION, CLOSENESS, HAPPINESS, AND INTIMACY. DECLARING INDEPENDENCE TO GAIN INTI-MACY MAY SEEM LIKE A DUMB THING TO DO, BUT IT CAN WORK VERY WELL.

A Little Structure Won't Kill Romance

Randy was a good-natured but controlling guy. He constantly ran over Sandra's opinions, interrupted her in conversations, and tended to take over the decision-making process. His dad had been that way, Randy took after him, and Sandra was pretty much ready to throw in the towel. I (John) told Randy, "The only way you'll get her to connect with you again is to humble yourself and give her room, space, and respect."

Remember my three rules for Randy? First, he couldn't say a word until Sandra finished telling him about a problem she had with him. Second, before stating his opinion, he had to let her know that he understood her experience. Third, he must agree to change anything that Sandra was right about. Only then could Randy talk about his side of the story. What values do these guidelines reflect? Why could following these guidelines actually enhance the romantic dimension of a relationship rather than stifle or even kill it?

_____

_____

_____

Which of these guidelines do you follow—naturally or with conscious effort—in your interactions with your lover? Which one(s) could you incorporate in order to better communicate with your lover?

_____

_____

_____

The Need for Relational Rules

All the understanding, patience, and grace in the world won't pull down a wall that arises when a lover is hurt and doesn't know what to do about it. It's like having a broken arm and hoping it will go away. All the good intentions in the world won't heal it until you get a cast to provide safety and structure, so the healing can happen. This is where relational rules and structure come into your love life. There are times when they are necessary to treat the wound. Like a cast on a broken limb, relational rules can preserve, protect, and even repair the love you want.

★ What was your initial reaction to the phrase *relational rules?* What does the metaphor of the cast help you appreciate about the value of relational rules?

★ What rules—unspoken or clearly defined—guide your love life? Give an example or two.

What recurring situation or pattern in your connection might benefit from relational rules? Here are some possibilities:

❑ Emotional unavailability
❑ Control
❑ Irresponsibility
❑ Defensiveness
❑ Chronic tardiness
❑ Overspending
❑ Unfaithfulness
❑ Rage

The behaviors just listed—and others as well—can bruise love and trust. They must be dealt with.

Not the Ideal, but the Real

Just as broken limbs aren't ideal, neither is having lots of rules for your relationship. Problems in connection are real though, and we need to accept the rules to deal with the problems.

One of the long-term goals of any love relationship is to have as few rules as possible. If you and your partner have made responsibility, care, sacrifice, and freedom parts of your normal behavior with each other, you don't need a lot of rules. You can trust your partner to act in your best interest, and you can rest in that. Love is sure to follow, as the environment is safe for it to grow and develop.

Remember the romantically faithful partner? His lover never needed to say, "I want you to make sure you're behaving appropriately with other women you meet at work." Rules that are lived don't need to be stated. Give an example of a rule that you and your lover are living.

_____

_____

_____

For what situation would you be wise to talk about and establish a rule? Be specific—or read on for some ideas.

_____

_____

_____

Think of rules as elements that protect and preserve. Use them when needed, and use as few as possible, so that freedom and love can flourish as much as possible.

When Do We Need Rules?

There are two criteria for the structure of rules. First, one of you is hurting the other and causing alienation and distance. Second, appeals to the offender on the basis of relationship aren't working.

Which aspect of your relationship, if any, do these criteria fit?

_____

_____

_____

Have you tried letting your lover know how the behavior affects you? Review this example: "That really hurt my feelings. I was trying to tell you that when you [fill in the blank], I go a million miles away from you." That kind of direct but not unloving statement is an appeal to the relationship: *what you are doing affects how I am feeling about you*. If you haven't yet, try this approach—and practice now. If you've tried this approach and nothing has changed, keep reading.

_____

_____

Ideally, the kind of statement just modeled will help your lover see himself through your eyes, feel sad that he has hurt you, and make the change. The two of you will reconnect, and love will go on. But sometimes the appeal is not enough. That is when you may need rules and structure.

★ "I've brought up the problem of [fill in the blank], but nothing is changing. And now your dismissing my feelings is becoming a big problem for me, bigger even than the [previously mentioned problem]. I think if you'd really understand how I am feeling, you would probably try to change. But since you're not hearing me, I am going to do this. For a while, if you dismiss my feelings and stop listening, I will just stop talking about it and solve the problem myself. But for a couple of days, I will just not be open at all to you. I won't be mean, but I won't be available or accessible. I don't like doing this, but my words aren't working. When you start trying to hear me again, I'll drop all this, but not until then." What was your initial reaction to these words? Is this a statement you could make? Why or why not?

_____

_____

_____

If you have not had a lot of experience setting limits, the suggested words may sound harsh or mean. But notice that this action was taken only when nothing else worked—and notice that it is about reconnecting, not punishment.

When reminders and appeals don't work toward solving a problem, you must impose structure. You will probably find lots of ways to address the details, but the point is, you need to call in external structures until the problem is solved. What kinds of structures might help you address the problem you're considering as you answer the questions in this section?

_____

_____

_____

Imposing rules is not meant as some sort of character diagnosis of your lover. Some people simply need experiences to make them aware of their effects on others when words don't work.

Next Steps

If your connection is being hurt by your lover's behavior or attitudes, and if words aren't working, call in the rules. Protect yourself and preserve the love you want to have.

BRING IN A THIRD PARTY. Seeing what the problem is, what exactly needs to change, what rules will help accomplish the change, how to deal with your own anxiety about the process—it is very difficult to do all this in your head. You need to borrow the head of a wise and trusted friend.

Whom can you and your lover talk with? What safe and responsible friend—who is for both of you and for the relationship—could you approach? Is your pastor a possibility? A counselor?

_____

_____

_____

BASE THE RULES ON RELATIONSHIP. When you decide what you are going to do, appeal to the connection. Make it clear that this is not about wanting to change or fix your lover. It is because you want to trust and love her, and you can't because of what she is doing. Always come back to the goal: *I am doing this because I want you, and I want us.*

State this goal in words that are your own, words that your lover will hear with the heart as well as the head.

_____

_____

_____

FOLLOW THROUGH. If rules are needed, set them and live them. If you are afraid you won't follow through, stop and get more resources and help, or you will make things worse for the two of you.

What will you do or whom will you find to help you be a firm but loving enforcer of the rules? Reminding yourself as well as your lover of the mantra is one possibility!

_____

_____

_____

A Lifeline: COMMIT AT THE OUTSET OF THE PROCESS TO HOLD ON TO YOUR STRUCTURE FOR THE ENTIRE TIME NEEDED. OFTEN, THE TIME WILL HELP YOUR LOVER EXPERIENCE YOUR FIRMNESS AND REALIZE THAT YOU ARE SERIOUS. AS HE COMES TO RECOGNIZE HIS NEED FOR YOU AND FOR YOUR GRACE, HE WILL BE MORE ABLE TO CHANGE HIS BEHAVIOR. KEEP THE RULES, GIVE GRACE, AND GIVE IT TIME. YOU'LL BE GLAD YOU DID.

Living What I Learn

Which of this section's four topics did you find most relevant or helpful? Explain.

❑ Trust Is a Risk You Have to Take
❑ Broken Trust Can Be Repaired
❑ Trust Thrives on Independence
❑ A Little Structure Won't Kill Romance

_____

_____

_____

★ Share one or two insights from the text that you found especially encouraging.

_____

_____

_____

Which of the following lifelines will you grab this week? What specific step(s) will you take to help rescue yourself and thereby rescue your marriage?

❏ Make risk, welcome, and trustworthiness a covenant in your connection with each other.

❏ Deal with trust problems with honesty, openness, and patience so that your relationship can heal and grow into a rewarding connection of trust and caring.

❏ Allow and exercise responsible freedom. Declare independence to gain intimacy.

❏ Keep the rules, give grace, and give it time. You'll be glad you did.

_____

_____

_____

As you close in prayer, ask God to help you see not only where you need to shore up trust but also how to do that. Identify one thing you can do either to show your trustworthiness to your partner or to take a small step toward learning to trust your mate again.

When you go to the meeting, be ready to . . .
- SHARE YOUR ANSWERS TO THE STARRED (★) QUESTIONS.
- CHOOSE WHICH OF THE LIFELINES YOU'LL GRAB AND WORK ON THIS WEEK.

During the week . . .
- AS YOU WORK ON YOUR SECTION 7 LIFELINE, PAY ATTENTION TO THE EFFECTS OF YOUR EFFORTS ON YOU, ON YOUR MATE, AND ON YOUR MARRIAGE.

DUMB ATTITUDE #8

"My Lover Should Be Perfect at Sex"

How can anything so wonderful, so sensational, so desirable, and so *fun* often go so wrong, as sex does? If you are among the couples who have encountered the downside of sex, we have good news for you. You can get the ecstasy back. You can restore the joy, the satisfaction, the love, and the sheer fun of sex.

What do you and your spouse know of the downside of sex—of it being a battleground or the scene of misery and despair?

_____

_____

_____

At this point, what do you see as the contributing factors?

_____

_____

What we offer here is not a sex manual; it's more of a hope manual. You will realize that, if you have sexual problems, you are not alone. We will help you identify the most common sexual problems so you will know how to address them. We will also tell you what kinds of help are available, giving you a point and a shove in the direction of healing.

If sex is the thing that needs rescue in your love life, here is the lifeboat that can bring you back to solid ground.

> *Dear God, I know that all good gifts come from You, and I know in my head that sex is a good gift that You've designed and given to married couples. Yet I know from experience that sex doesn't always seem like much of a gift. You know our struggles; You know our heartache. Please bring healing to me, to us, and to our relationship. The joy, satisfaction, love, and sheer fun of sex—what gifts those would be! I believe; help my unbelief. In Jesus's name. Amen.*

Good Sex Doesn't Just Happen

What is healthy sex? It depends on whom you ask. Sex is a very individual topic with opinions varying from person to person and relationship to relationship.

★ What was your sense of "healthy sex" before you were married—and what were the sources of that idea?

_____

_____

_____

Sex is important and powerful. It has the power to do many good things for the marriage partners as well as for the relationship. And when it is not going well in some way, sex has its own set of threats.

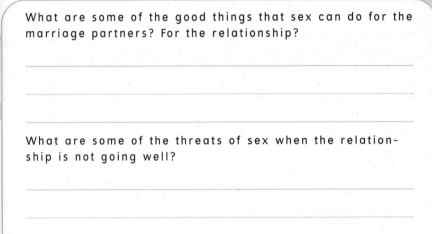

What are some of the good things that sex can do for the marriage partners? For the relationship?

What are some of the threats of sex when the relationship is not going well?

In light of the high and honorable place God has reserved for sex, and in light of the pleasure and pain it can bring, it is good to look past Hugh Hefner and *Cosmopolitan* to determine what good, healthy sex really is. You need to know, for it is an important part of preserving and reestablishing your connection.

Healthy Sex Knows Best

From the Creator's view, sex is the ultimate expression of *knowing* someone. That is why it is not something casual or unimportant. On the contrary, sex is the deepest expression of intimacy and of knowing another person.

What do you find interesting about, first, the fact that the Bible's word for "having sex" comes from the Hebrew word that means "to know"? And, second, about the fact

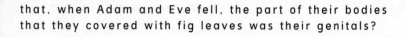

that, when Adam and Eve fell, the part of their bodies that they covered with fig leaves was their genitals?

Shame, inadequacy, fear, guilt, and disconnection had all gotten in the way of Adam and Eve's ability to be known at the deepest levels of who they were. What shame, inadequacy, fear, guilt, or disconnection gets in the way of you and your mate being known by each other?

First and foremost, healthy sex is sex that expresses *knowing one another in the deepest sort of intimacy with the absence of fear, shame, hurt, or guilt.* Sex is where total vulnerability is expressed; it is a knowing of the other person's heart, mind, soul, and strength. Let's look at some of the things that help couples truly know each other in the deepest biblical, or sexual, ways.

Healthy Sex Is Connected Sex

Jason was only making love to Amanda's body and not the rest of her. He was "making sex," not love. So they began to work on it.

Merriam-Webster's Dictionary gives a three-part definition of sex that actually works as three steps toward more connected sex. What are the three definitions of *intercourse* in Webster's (Book pg. 226)? And, yes, the order matters!

Do you and your lover generally take these three steps in order? What are the consequences of doing so—or not doing so?

Men, what does this three-part definition of *intercourse* alert you to? And, women, what insight into sex does this definition give you?

As Jason and Amanda started talking more, they began to share other things that were on their minds, and this verbal intercourse turned into a deep knowing that led to sexual intercourse that now was not only mental, but also much more physical than they had ever known. In the end, Jason got more of what he had been looking for in the beginning, but not by getting physical first. He found that the physical followed the connection. After all, good sex is connected sex—sex between a connected couple.

Healthy Sex Is Freely Given

Healthy sex is sex where both parties feel like they are there, in the act, by their own choosing.

Love is something that is freely given. If a person feels controlled into giving sex, it is no longer love but slavery. If "one" stands for "slavery" and "ten" for "free to give and receive love," what rank would you give your sex life?

Explain why you gave the ranking you did—and remember as you do so that virtually all sexual problems can be fixed.

When people are free to engage in sex voluntarily, they can be truly "there." So an important aspect of connecting with each other sexually is talking about the degree of freedom that each of you feels in saying no either to having sex at any particular time or to participating in any particular aspect of sex.

Just as other areas of your relationship will display different preferences, desires, and leanings, so will sex. Were you surprised to learn this? Comment on your initial realization of this fact and the effect it had on your marriage.

You will have different tastes in what you desire and enjoy sexually. Here is the key: *in good relationships, lovers do not view these preferences as a problem, but as natural.* What can you do to normalize in your mind and/or emotions the fact that you and your lover have different sexual tastes?

★ In good relationships, as in the rest of life, the two lovers listen, understand, and compromise to give to each other in ways that are the most satisfying for each. Neither one gets left behind. What, if anything, makes it hard for you and your lover to come to a compromise in the area of sex?

Compromise means giving sometimes when it would not be your preference, as an act of love. Compromise also means doing without sometimes when it would not be your preference, also as an act of love. Lovers both give freedom and act out of freedom. That is what it means to truly *know* each other.

Healthy Sex Is Accepting Sex

Good sex is not expert sex, but rather sex where both people feel accepted, right where they are—and where the relationship feels OK, right where it is, at whatever level of sexual health or competency it has. *Good sex is "failure-free" sex.*

★ What unreal standards for "good" sex do you have for yourself, thereby setting yourself up for "failure"?

What unreal standards for "good" sex do you have for your lover, thereby setting him or her up for "failure" and yourself up for disappointment or frustration?

_____

_____

_____

Give each other the freedom to not get it right. Give your relationship the freedom to fail sometimes. Some of the most sexually satisfied couples report that they moved from the fear of things not going well to the ability to laugh together at those times when it just wasn't working.

Healthy sex comes out of a total acceptance, not only of failures but also of each other's personhood, bodies, and the rest of what makes you who you are. First of all, where, if at all, do you struggle to accept your own personhood, body, and the rest of what makes you who you are? What will you do about that struggle?

_____

_____

_____

Where, if at all, do you struggle to accept your lover—your lover's personhood, body, and the rest of what makes your lover who he/she is? What will you do about this struggle?

_____

_____

_____

If you want a great sex life, then work on accepting each other in all areas of life. Get judgment, performance anxiety, guilt, lack of forgiveness, and other unrealistic expectations out of your relationship—and out of your sex life.

Healthy Sex Is Fun

Healthy sex involves knowing *all* of each other—body, heart, mind, soul, and strength. And part of that is the physical act itself.

Review the discussions of "soulish" sex, intellectual sex, and physical sex (Book pgs. 228-229). There is physical sex that is simply passion, desire, and the coming together of two people as "one flesh." Do you need permission to let sex be simply a moment of pure, physical fun? If so, consider permission granted! Have fun, and get physical.

But remember this: couples who enjoy times where sex is just fun and physical have that because all the other more connecting aspects are in place. What connecting aspects in your relationship could use some reinforcements—and what will you do to strengthen those weaker links?

If your heart's connection is secure, and you and your spouse are really "knowing" each other in all the ways we have talked about, you can have fun, physical sex and no one gets hurt. Safety and connection are already there, so you are free to be physical.

Healthy Sex Requires Communicating

Couples with the greatest satisfaction are those who talk to each other about sex—about their wants, desires, likes, dislikes, fears, pains, insecurities, and whatever else comes into the picture. These couples have a safe space just to get to know each other sexually, apart from having sex.

Are you and your lover able to get to know each other sexually apart from having sex? If so, what benefits have you enjoyed because of that effort? If not, what might you do to make that part of your connection?

_____

_____

_____

Comment on the statement "Talking is imperative to healthy sex." Then note any obstacles that keep you and your lover from doing just that. What, for instance, needs to happen for you to create a safe place for talking without criticism or judgment about the things listed above? What needs to happen to make it OK to communicate openly without either of you taking what is said personally?

_____

_____

_____

Remember, the goal of sex is to know each other better, and to do that you need the safety to talk.

"Knowing" Each Other Is a Process

Sex means to "know" someone, and you must remember that it takes time to know a person. Healthy sex is just like any other aspect of your relationship: it takes time to build.

★ Couples with healthy sex lives give each other time to get to know each other. They never assume they know everything about themselves or each other and are always learning. They allow the necessary time to be sure the right things happen. What can you do to make getting to know each other a higher priority in your life? Try to take one step toward that goal this week.

A Lifeline: WE ALL DEAL WITH WORK, KIDS, PERSONAL PRESSURES, AND LIFE ISSUES. DESPITE ALL THAT FILLS OUR SCHEDULE AND DRAINS OUR ENERGY, WE HAVE TO GIVE SEX TIME AND SPACE SO THAT IT GETS THE ATTENTION IT DESERVES IN OUR MARRIAGE. IF YOU INVEST TIME IN GROWING TOGETHER AND KEEP WORKING ON YOUR SEX LIFE, THE RETURNS WILL BE WORTH IT ALL.

Untangling the "Nots" in Unhealthy Sex

Let's review some of the ingredients that create healthy sex:
- Knowing each other
- Being connected
- Being free
- Being accepting
- Having fun
- Communicating
- Seeing sex as a process

★ What new insight into healthy sex does this list give you? What motivation for improving your love life do you find here?

_____

_____

_____

Which one of these ingredients is firmly in place for you and your lover? Be thankful and encouraged.

_____

_____

_____

Which item have you chosen to work on first—and what step(s) have you decided to take?

_____

_____

_____

If those are the ingredients for healthy sex, then what are the ingredients of unhealthy sex? Answer: the absence of those same things. Let's take a look at the other side of healthy sex for a moment, so you can rid your relationship of the dynamics that destroy your connection in the sexual arena and beyond.

Not Knowing or Connecting

If "being known" is what sex is about, then the *absence* of being known is unhealthy sex. Unhealthy or disconnected sex occurs when one of the partners is not relating to his mate as a whole person, but he still wants sex. He takes no time to find out where his mate's heart, mind, soul, or strength is; he wants to have sex that is disconnected from the rest of the person.

Women, if you are familiar with disconnected sex, what keeps your heart from participating in the act?

_____

_____

_____

Men, if you are participating in disconnected sex, why are you choosing to connect only with your body and not with your heart, mind, or emotions?

_____

_____

_____

If you are feeling like a sex object or that your physical relationship is without heart and soul, then it is time to talk about it—and about your fears, hurts, needs, desires, and the like. Why aren't those parts of you not coming into the relationship—and what will you do to bring them in?

_____

_____

_____

_____

Agree to have sex only when you are both feeling like you are heard, understood, and connected with each other. Then, working together, come up with a strategy for having your physical connection be equal to your relational connection. That will be good for both of you.

Not Being Free

Remember, you must have freedom to have love. So if one of you is putting pressure on the other, controlling the other into having more sex than he or she wants, or having some kind of sex that he or she doesn't want, that is not healthy. Couples must talk through such differences and negotiate, compromising and sacrificing. That is normal.

It is unhealthy when those sacrifices are made against a partner's will—when the pressure of personality, manipulation, guilt, or something else causes one partner to go past where he or she feels comfortable going. To what degree is this unhealthiness present in your relationship?

Talk about this issue. Talk about the freedom that exists in your relationship to say no easily and simply, as in, "Not tonight, please. I'm tired." Are you free to say no to sex just as you would say no to anything else you didn't want at the moment? If so, why do you hesitate to say no to sex? If not, move on to the next question.

If you don't feel free to say no to sex, the problem may be coming from your own head, or it may be a dynamic between the two of you. Sometimes you cannot know which until you talk it out. Likewise, it is important to talk about what you agree to do or not do sexually. Make sure the agreements are not due to pressure or coercion of any kind. How will you approach your mate on this subject?

You must have freedom to have love. At the same time, if freedom is exercised without concern for the other person's needs, then love loses as well. To just say no to everything and not consider your mate's sexual needs or desires is not loving either. That is taking advantage of freedom. So, balance the two: freedom and love.

One more thought about freedom. If there are control dynamics in your relationship, chances are that your sex life is going to be affected. Women, does your husband feel controlled by you? If so, what behaviors, statements, and attitudes are causing this—if you don't know, ask!—and what steps will you take to change them?

Men, if you are feeling controlled by your wife and therefore less attracted to her sexually, determine how you will speak that truth to her in love. With what behaviors, statements, attitudes, and relational patterns is she controlling you? Be specific and, again, speak the truth in love.

Make freedom one of your highest goals in your relationship (Galatians 5:1).

Not Being Accepting

Few dynamics cause more sexual dysfunction than the lack of acceptance. Good sexual response requires the lack of tension, and performance anxiety causes tension. Obviously, the two are incompatible. One of the most helpful things that a sex

therapist does is cure impotence by just getting rid of performance anxiety. It can be that simple, but it seems like such a
miracle. In short, *no one should ever have to worry about not
being "good enough." That is a sex killer.*

What aspect(s) of your spouse do you need to be more
accepting of? Not accepting your lover's body, the way
he makes love, or other aspects of his personhood can
all put him under a shame dynamic, giving him feelings
of inadequacy and lead to problems in the bedroom.

What aspect(s) of you would you like your mate to be
more accepting of? With what words will you speak that
truth in love?

There is nothing wrong with talking about ways that each of you
wants the other to do things differently. But there is everything
wrong if that is done in a critical, shaming, or judgmental way.

Take an inventory to see how you are making requests
with each other. Is there a hint of disapproval, anger, guilt,
shame, or comparison in your voice or body language?
Are you implying a loss of love or connection because of
something about your partner's performance? It is great
to be talking with your partner about this, but you have
to watch the way that you talk.

How accepted do you feel by the other? How can you give requests or feedback in a way that does not hurt, apply pressure, or become deflating?

In a healthy love life, there *must* be acceptance of the bad stuff—each other's fears, feelings, fantasies, desires, hurts, inadequacies, weaknesses, past, or whatever else is lurking in between one's heart and the connection—as well as the good. Accepting everything about each other is part of a formula for healthy and good sex.

Self-acceptance also affects sexual health. What about yourself, if anything, do you tend to reject (your own body, desires, sexuality, or other aspects of yourself)?

Listen to the way that you talk to yourself, especially during lovemaking. Are you critical of yourself? Are you evaluating yourself in some way? You must shut down that voice and move toward acceptance. What steps could you take to become more accepting of yourself? What step will you begin with?

Self-acceptance also affects sexual health. Lack of it can really get in the way of sexual expression. Working toward self-acceptance will improve your sex life.

Not Having Fun

Sex should be fun. But for some couples, sex becomes routine, a duty, or an obligation; and that is unhealthy.

If your sex life is lacking in spontaneity, freedom, and enjoyment, then something is wrong. What personal hurt or injury, if any, needs to be understood and healed? What rigid religious teaching or parental messages do you need to rework?

★ Read together (ideally!) the Song of Solomon in the Bible, one of the most explicit descriptions of marital sex ever recorded. What new appreciation about God's gift of sex do those passionate verses give you?

Obligations and inhibitions are unhealthy to good sex. Both partners need more freedom so the joy can return to the bedroom (or wherever you happen to be).

Not Communicating

Sadly, many couples are afraid to really talk about what they want or don't want in their sex life. As a result, they are doomed to stay stuck, as each partner has no way of knowing what the other really wants.

If you are not having verbal intercourse, then your sexual intercourse is sure to be lacking as well. Why you aren't communicating about sex? Is one of you reactive? Defensive? Judgmental? Moralistic? Does one of you take things personally? Is one of you unable to accept feedback? If those dynamics are at play, talk about them as they relate to sex.

Whatever is in the way of your communication, what are some specific and practical steps you can take to get it out of the way? Or whom will you talk to for help in defining a course of action?

Maybe your communication failures are not about the relationship at all, but about your own fears of being open. Why are you afraid to talk? Look at those fears and face them. Your sex life will benefit from that kind of risk-taking.

Not Seeing Sex As a Process

You can't hurry sex. If there is the pressure in your sexual relationship to have it all together right now, you need an attitude adjustment that makes sex more like a journey together, with total safety and lack of time pressure to get there.

Is either of you feeling pressure to have your sex life all together right now? If so, why?

★ Sex is a trip of discovery, pleasure, self-knowledge, other-knowledge, and adventure. What is your reaction to the truth that you are never going to "arrive," but you will learn more and more about each other and how to make better love until the day that "death does [you] part"? In what ways might this truth affect your love life?

There is the microcosm version of that same truth. Just as you have to give yourselves time over the course of your relationship to get it right, you also have to give yourselves time in any one sexual encounter. What, if anything, keeps you from taking time when you are with your lover—and what will you do about those factors that hurry you too much?

Give yourselves the time it takes to get relaxed, pleasured, loved, connected, and the like. Sex is not a race.

False Sexual Expectations

Another way that sex can become unhealthy is when it faces false expectations. Sex cannot lead the relationship, for example. Sex cannot *be* the entire relationship, as many magazines and movies ask it to be. The frequency or kinds of orgasms one is supposed to experience, or the longevity or intensity of the experience—these are not the criteria for evaluating a love life. The truth is that sex is very individual, and every person and every relationship is different.

What expectations from the media, friends' reports of their sexual experiences, or magazine articles that blow things out of reality do you need to ignore?

What false expectations for sex does your lover seem to have?

Your sexual performance, aside from real dysfunction, is your sexual performance. Your relationship is your relationship. The only standard that is important is your own satisfaction and fulfillment with each other. Let reality be good enough, and let loving each other be the real expectation you try to meet.

The Good News About Unhealthy Sex

The good news about unhealthy sex is that it can be helped. If you struggle with sexual issues, then we encourage you to get help from a qualified sex therapist. Chances are good that he or she can help you greatly.

What hesitations, if any, do you have about seeking help from a sex therapist?

What truths—about the value of therapy or the importance of healthy sex in your marriage or the truth that sex is God's gift to you—can you counter those objections with?

_____

_____

_____

The really good news is that sexual problems are resolved in tandem with relationship problems. The things we have talked about here all have to do with improving your relationship as well as your sex life.

A Lifeline: WORKING ON YOUR SEX LIFE IS A GREAT PLACE TO FOCUS ON REBUILDING YOUR CONNECTION, AS IT GETS INTO SO MANY AREAS OF FINDING EACH OTHER AGAIN. GET STARTED!

Keep the Home Fires Burning

Hollywood depictions of the sexual moment may be engaging to watch, but they lead many couples to expect that all they need for a fulfilling sexual relationship is moonlight, a little breeze, and the right music in the background. The movies never show the couple five years later, three kids later, fifty-hour workweeks later, forty pounds later, or any of the other "laters" that make for real life.

What "laters" are you and your lover facing these days?

_____

_____

_____

In what ways, if any, have those "laters" affected your sexual connection?

_____

_____

_____

_____

Sustaining a fulfilling sexual connection in your marriage takes focus, attention, and work. The good news, though, is that anything worth having takes effort, and the effort is worth it in the end. In this chapter, we will give you a few tips on how to keep your sex life alive and healthy.

Talk, Talk, Talk

We simply cannot overemphasize how important talking is to your sexual connection. You've got to talk!

Read through the following list of topics to talk about. Mark ones that you need to talk about with your lover. Choose the top three or five and rank them. Then make a date to talk!

❑ How do you feel about your sex life? How would you like your sex life to be different?

❑ What are your areas of insecurity?

❑ What areas would you like to explore?

❑ How do you feel about your foreplay, and how do you want it to be different?

❑ What does your mate do that you really like and wish he would do more of?

❑ What does your mate do that you don't like and wish he would not do?

❑ How do you feel inhibited, and what could your mate do to make you feel less so?

❑ What positions do you like, don't like, or would like to try?

❑ What makes it hard for you to communicate about sex?

❑ What fantasies do you have that you want your mate to fulfill?

❑ What fears do you have about sex?

❑ What makes you tense?

❑ What makes you relaxed?

❑ What turns you on before sex and makes you begin to desire your mate?

❑ What do you want your mate to know that you feel like he doesn't know?

❑ What attitudes, actions, and words would help you to feel safer and more fulfilled?

Be nonjudgmental so that you are safe to talk freely without hearing each other's comments as criticism. If you can't get to that safe place with each other, that indicates another problem, and you need to talk to a counselor.

Become Self-Aware

Sometimes your own feelings about sex or about yourself stand in the way of your responsiveness. Both men and women who experience sexual arousal or performance problems have thoughts that lead to those symptoms.

★ Which, if any, of the following are getting in the way of your sexual connection with your spouse?

❑ Beliefs

❑ Self-talk

❑ Guilt

❑ Thought life about sex and during sex

★ What will you do to change these patterns and beliefs that are interfering? You could start by talking to your mate, a good friend, or a counselor.

_____

_____

_____

Also, become more aware of your own body and sensations. What turns you on, and what makes you feel safe? What things make you feel tense or nervous?

_____

_____

_____

What aspects of your self-image are negative and inhibiting? What will you do to develop a healthier self-image?

_____

_____

_____

There is nothing wrong with learning about your own body— what makes it tick, how your body relaxes, and how it is aroused. So take a warm bath and learn to feel your body. Touch yourself, and find out what feels good and where your most sensual feelings are. Share those discoveries with your mate, and instruct him or her about your body and your feelings.

notes:

Have Nonsexual Sensual Exercises

One of the most important things that sex therapists have couples do is nonintercourse, or nongenital, pleasuring exercises. This involves making a rule of either not having genital-to-genital contact, or no genital contact at all.

Review the following five reasons that sensate focus or nonintercourse pleasuring exercises are helpful. (These are discussed more completely on Book pgs. 240–241.)

- SENSATE FOCUS TAKES THE PERFORMANCE PRESSURE OFF. The idea is to pleasure your mate, and there is no way to fail.

- SENSATE FOCUS ALLOWS YOU TO GET IN TOUCH WITH YOUR BODY. It helps you find out what feels good, erotic, relaxing, intimate, connecting, and the like.

- SENSATE FOCUS IS A CONNECTING EXPERIENCE IN AND OF ITSELF. It is connection without sex as opposed to sex without connection.

- SENSATE FOCUS EDUCATES EACH PARTNER ABOUT THE OTHER. You will learn things that you did not know that your mate feels, likes, and dislikes.

- SENSATE FOCUS TRAINS MEN TO SLOW DOWN THEIR TENDENCY TO PUSH TOWARD THE GOAL. And when they do, they often find that she really is sensual, responsive, and even erotic after all.

Which of these reasons is reason enough for you to spend some time having nonsexual sensual experiences with your lover?

_____

_____

_____

What date to do so will you put on your calendar?

_____

Kill Evaluation

There are few bigger desire and performance killers, as we have said, than evaluation and performance anxiety.

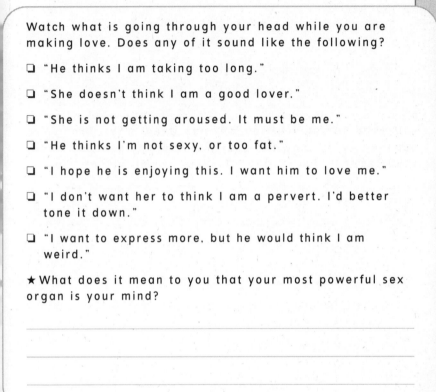

Watch what is going through your head while you are making love. Does any of it sound like the following?

❏ "He thinks I am taking too long."

❏ "She doesn't think I am a good lover."

❏ "She is not getting aroused. It must be me."

❏ "He thinks I'm not sexy, or too fat."

❏ "I hope he is enjoying this. I want him to love me."

❏ "I don't want her to think I am a pervert. I'd better tone it down."

❏ "I want to express more, but he would think I am weird."

★ What does it mean to you that your most powerful sex organ is your mind?

Don't allow sex-killing evaluation to be in your mind. Stop evaluating and begin experiencing. Get into the moment and feel it. Focus on it. Talk about it, but don't judge. That only leads to fear and shame.

Sex Begins in the Kitchen

Sex does not begin when you begin "sex." It is an outgrowth of the connection, love, and tenderness that you have shown up to that moment. That moment is only a culmination of what's already going on.

Women, what can you do to begin sex sooner? That may mean not nagging, controlling, or judging. Which of those, if any, do you need to be more careful to avoid— and what specific positive steps can you take to begin sex sooner?

_____

_____

_____

Men, what can you do to begin sex sooner? What will you do to pursue your lover in nonsexual ways through- out the day, to show her that you want to know her mind, soul, feelings, heart, and interests as well as her body?

_____

_____

_____

In short, be loving, kind, tender, initiating, and helpful in the kitchen, over the phone, throughout the day—and chances are, she'll make you glad you did.

Eliminate Pressure

Pressure of any kind works against everything that sex is designed to do. Get performance pressure out of your bedroom—and out of your relationship.

If he is not erect or it takes time to get there, what will you do to make that OK? If she is not getting aroused, what will you do to make that OK?

_____

_____

_____

Men, above all else, *slow down*. Remember—or teach yourself—that foreplay is a very important part of good sex. Why do you tend to want to hurry things along? What can you do to slow yourself down?

_____

_____

_____

Women need to be close and aroused slowly to get to desire. Men get desire first and then move to being close. This is good in that it makes the man the pursuer, leading the woman to feel wanted and loved. It is God's design.

Women, what standards for your arousal or your climax have you established for yourself? What steps will you take to release those standards—for good?

_____

_____

_____

Ladies, what do you do—or could you do—during and/or after sex to stroke your lover's fragile male ego? What compliments do—or could—you offer him? What will you say or do to show him you like being with him, being there, wanting him, or whatever you feel? For starters, smile!

_____

_____

_____

The bottom line here is that sex is about a relaxed, emotional, loving, relational, and physical response. You are a team to pleasure each other, not perform for each other or judge each other or even judge yourselves. By all means, if you can't solve these issues, see a good sex counselor for help.

Get Physical

Research shows that people in better physical condition have better sex.

What will you do in each of the following categories? Be specific, get moving, and have someone hold you accountable or, better yet, join you!

· Get in shape

· Eat healthy

· Get more rest

· Cut down on stress

All of these disciplines have been shown to improve sex. So get a buddy system, hire a trainer, or join a class. Whatever it takes, do it.

Make Time

Loving takes time and space. If you're doing it as an afterthought—with whatever few minutes and little energy are left at the end of the day—that will be the quality of your love life.

What will you do to be proactive about each of the following aspects of your love life?

❏ Make time. Schedule it. Mark your calendar now!

❑ Vary it. What will you do to add a little spice?

_____

_____

❑ Go on overnighters. Find a weekend in the next two months and get away!

❑ Have a date night that does not get tinkered with short of emergencies. Which night can be date night for you?

_____

_____

❑ Have sex appointments. So it doesn't sound romantic. So what? Make an "appointment" today!

However you do it, make protected time for making love.

Support Each Other

Remember, you are one flesh; when one of you struggles, both of you struggle. So get with each other and bring each other along.

With what is your lover struggling? And what will you do to support him or her?

_____

_____

_____

What are you struggling with? Does your lover know about the struggle—and what kind of support you would like? If not, talk!

_____

_____

_____

Loyally supporting and accepting each other in all situations is a move toward better lovemaking. Supporting each other in any struggle you may have will strengthen your connection with each other.

We have tried to give you some time- and research-tested information that should prove helpful in your relationship. But, don't stop here.

What point discussed in this section do you want to learn more about?

_____

_____

Where will you go to find helpful information?

_____

_____

What issue has you thinking about seeing a counselor or a sex therapist? When will you take that step?

_____

_____

A Lifeline: BECOMING A STUDENT OF GOOD SEX IN MARRIAGE, AS WELL AS A STUDENT OF EACH OTHER AND YOURSELF, IS ONE OF THE HEALTHIEST THINGS YOU CAN DO TO RESCUE YOUR LOVE LIFE.

Unfaithfulness Is More
than Just Adultery

Satisfying sexuality goes much deeper than looks or mechan-
ics, and research attributes it to the quality of the connection
between the couple. How well do they listen, tend to each
other's needs, see sex as another way to know each other, and
feel safe and free to be all of who they are with each other?

> Which of these four aspects of sexuality do you think your
> lover most wants you to work on? If you're not sure, ask.
>
> _____
>
> _____
>
> Which of these four aspects of sexuality do you most
> want your lover to work on? What will you say to
> communicate that desire?
>
> _____
>
> _____

In this section on rekindling your sex life, we will address one
of the biggest things that destroy it: *taking your sexuality
outside the marriage.* Since sexual fulfillment is about total
connection, then taking parts of yourself outside your marriage
for sexual gratification is certainly an enemy of that fulfillment.

> There are many ways of taking sex outside marriage, the
> obvious one being an affair. We've already discussed
> resisting the temptation to have an affair, so we will not

dwell on that issue in this section. But review the section on bringing out the worst (Book pg. 115) if you're dealing with the temptation or the aftermath of an affair.

_____

_____

_____

The Cycle of Sexual Addiction

There are other ways besides affairs in which people take their sexuality outside of the marriage.

Which of these three presents the greatest temptation to you?

❑ Pornography
❑ Romantic novels or videos
❑ Fantasy crushes on other people

While people who engage in these practices are not having an actual affair, they are taking sexual parts of themselves in directions other than their mates. When a partner turns to pornography, for instance, the parts of him that engage in the activity run from the marriage. These activities may not have all of the same repercussions as physical adultery, but they still defile the person and the relationship, as Jesus and any good marriage therapist will tell you (Matthew 5:28).

★ People turn to pornography, romantic novels or videos, and crushes for a variety of reasons. Which of the following makes those forbidden fruits appealing to you?

❑ Fears
❑ Conflicts

❏ Feeling overpowered in the relationship
❏ Feeling inadequate
❏ Feeling criticized
❏ Being afraid of intimacy
❏ Something else?

★ What did you learn from the discussion of fantasy relationships (Book pgs. 247–249)? The discussion of addiction to pornography (Book pgs. 247–249)?

When a partner is involved in pornography, romantic novels or videos, or fantasy relationships, the marriage is the victim. So are both partners. Intimacy suffers, walls are built, sexual desire goes away, interest vanishes, and isolation ensues.

What to Do

If this cycle of addiction describes you, get help. Do not think that you are just going to stop this addiction through will power. You need God's help and the help of others who understand sexual addiction to help you get out. Call a counselor with experience in sexual addiction or go to a group such as Sexaholics Anonymous or other recovery groups designed for this kind of problem. Sexual addiction can certainly be overcome, but you need help to make it happen.

Which of these steps will you take this week? Whom will you ask to hold you accountable to taking this initial step and to following through on your efforts to find healing and freedom?

If this describes your spouse, put your foot down. Set some boundaries. Tell her that you are not going to share her with someone else, even a fantasized person. Tell her that you want all of her, and you want your marriage to work. Tell her that you will deal with anything about yourself that has made it difficult for her to come to you, and you will help her deal with anything that might be causing fear or pain. Make it clear that what you will not do is continue to pretend that there is not a problem and enable it to go on.

Which of these steps will you take this week to help your spouse, your marriage, yourself? If you make the appointment and your spouse will not go, go yourself to figure out with a professional the correct stance to take. Do not just allow the behavior to go on. Pray for her and get others praying as well. This can be overcome.

If neither you nor your spouse has this problem, don't think it could not happen to you.

★ What does Proverbs 16:18 say—and what is the significance of this truth in the context of this discussion of sexual faithfulness?

Describe your spiritual accountability and growth support system. To whom are confessing all of your temptations? From whom is nothing hidden?

If you don't have such a system in place, list some of the benefits that it could offer you. Then come up with a plan to establish such accountability and support in your life.

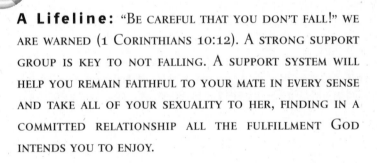

A Lifeline: "BE CAREFUL THAT YOU DON'T FALL!" WE ARE WARNED (1 CORINTHIANS 10:12). A STRONG SUPPORT GROUP IS KEY TO NOT FALLING. A SUPPORT SYSTEM WILL HELP YOU REMAIN FAITHFUL TO YOUR MATE IN EVERY SENSE AND TAKE ALL OF YOUR SEXUALITY TO HER, FINDING IN A COMMITTED RELATIONSHIP ALL THE FULFILLMENT GOD INTENDS YOU TO ENJOY.

Facing Sexual Dysfunction

This section has two purposes. The first is to educate you about sexual dysfunctions that are very common with normal people. The second is to give you hope and motivation to face your problem and get help. The key is to stop minimizing your problem and its effect on your marriage, and get help from a seasoned professional. The results can be amazing, and your marriage will benefit.

★ What problem in the area of sex are you and your lover currently struggling with? Be honest about your problem, and deal with it directly. That's the first step toward healing and freedom.

_____

_____

_____

Does a sense of shame, fear, guilt, or something else keep you from honestly facing the problem? From making plans to overcome it? What can you do about that barrier to healing?

_____

_____

Once you've acknowledged the problem, will you locate good self-help books and/or work with a trained sex therapist? Don't struggle needlessly with sexual dysfunction.

_____

_____

Since sex is a very personal issue, many couples simply hide and avoid dealing with sexual dysfunction. Don't choose that option. If you are solidly on each other's team and *for* each other, if you are willing to extend total love and acceptance of each other's hurts and weaknesses, you can get past the problem. We say, "Go for it!"

Common Sexual Dysfunctions

Here are some of the most common sexual problems.

LACK OR LOSS OF SEX DRIVE. Many couples find themselves at some time or another in a situation where one of them experiences a lack of sex drive.

If this is an issue for you or your lover, and you two are feeling very positive and loving toward each other, investigate biological or medical causes. Hormonal changes, depression, drug interactions or side effects, diabetes, stress, or other medical illnesses can cause sex drive to wane or disappear. You may have a perfectly logical biological cause that can be easily treated.

Lack of sex drive can also result from relational or psychological issues. Which of the following might be a factor?

❏ The dynamics of the relationship
❏ One partner's psychological dynamics
❏ Self-image problems
❏ Hurts from the past that are not healed
❏ Reminders of problems with their parents

A good therapist can help identify and then treat those problems quite effectively. We encourage you to get that help.

IMPOTENCE. Impotence is the inability to achieve or maintain an erection for intercourse. It is one of life's most painful emotional experiences for men, and it is often frustrating for their wives as well. It is not uncommon for the woman to blame herself for not being exciting enough or to feel responsible for making it better somehow. So it puts a lot of strain on both partners.

The causes of impotence can be either physical or emotional. Get the medical aspect of it checked first. Contact your physician before you do anything else.

Psychological, emotional, and relational causes for impotence are not uncommon either. Performance anxiety may contribute to impotence. Consider such underlying factors.

Whatever the cause of impotence, proven treatments are available. So don't put it off another day: get help from a qualified doctor or counselor.

AVOIDANCE OF SEX. At times when the relationship is strained, one or both parties may avoid initiating or agreeing to sex. If that is the case, it's generally because someone is hurting in some way.

If one of you is avoiding sex, which of the following might be contributing to that?

❑ Your lover is hurting
❑ Unhealed abuse issues
❑ Inhibitions
❑ Guilt
❑ Repressive spiritual or religious teachings
❑ Parental messages
❑ Addictions
❑ Fear

❏ Shame

❏ Something else?

Talk with your mate about these things to get a handle on whether you need to work through an issue with your relationship or find help for a personal issue.

_____

_____

_____

Even if it is a personal issue, it is also a relational issue because it affects your mate, and his help and support are going to be important.

PREMATURE EJACULATION. Premature ejaculation is also a great source of distress for both the man and woman. The good news is that premature ejaculation is very treatable, even with do-it-yourself treatment.

Like other sexual problems, premature ejaculation can be relational, psychological, or medical. You would do well to consult your doctor first to rule out medical conditions.

_____

_____

_____

If you've ruled out medical conditions, will you next turn to a good sex therapy book for some self-help ideas? Or will you find a good sex therapist?

_____

_____

_____

You and your mate should work on this together with the same kind of sensitivity and support that you would give each other with any problem.

RETARDED EJACULATION. Retarded ejaculation is a problem that many men do not even know exists, and when it appears, they wonder what is wrong. Like other sexual problems, it can put lots of strain on the relationship.

Again, talk to your doctor first to get a good physical diagnosis. Certain medical conditions and certain medications can cause retarded ejaculation.

If the doctor gives you a clean bill of health, seek sex therapy.

Many men who have this problem are able to ejaculate when masturbating, but not during intercourse. There are sex therapy techniques that can overcome the problem, whether it is relational or psychological.

VAGINISMUS. Vaginismus is a disorder that makes penetration of the vagina impossible because of an involuntary contraction. It closes, and nothing is able to penetrate. Like other sexual problems, vaginismus can be caused by physical conditions or relational and psychological factors.

• First explore possible medical causes for vaginismus.
• Learn exercises from a good sex therapy book or a counselor.

• Be open to more extensive sex therapy if necessary.

If you suffer from vaginismus, don't wait; get help. It's available and it works.

ORGASMIC DYSFUNCTION. As we said earlier, in more than half the cases, women need additional stimulation other than intercourse in order to reach orgasm.

Husbands, assignment number one is to provide for her stimulation in addition to intercourse. There is no right way that works for every woman, and you can have a great time finding what works for you.

_____

_____

Orgasmic dysfunction can also be caused by emotional, psychological, or relational pressures. What will you do, first, to identify these pressures and, second, to relieve them?

_____

_____

The orgasm is a "letting-go" response, and a woman is wired to let go when she is in a relaxed and safe place. Anything internal or external that makes her anxious or causes her to feel under pressure, afraid, or uncomfortable can work against her. What dynamics in your relationship, if any, may be triggering these tensions?

_____

_____

_____

Sex therapy for orgasmic dysfunction can be very helpful, and we recommend it. If you take advantage of the help that is widely available, not only will your love life improve, but your overall health will improve as well.

Get Together

Where there is love, there is a way. Couples who are committed to being for each other and for the relationship can overcome huge obstacles or, in the case of sexual dysfunction, very curable obstacles that only feel huge.

★Obstacles to good sexual connection feel huge because sexuality is a point of vulnerability for both men and women. Furthermore, a lot of feelings are wrapped up in one's view of oneself and one's performance. What might you do to make these obstacles seem less huge, more manageable, even conquerable?

_____

_____

_____

★Why do we suggest that the term *performance* be dropped from your sexual vocabulary?

_____

_____

_____

A Lifeline: Only love and safety can help a couple out of the performance trap and into what sex is meant to be: a deeper way of *knowing* each other. If you need help to get there, by all means, get that help. Your sex life—and your love life—will thank you for it.

Living What I Learn

Which of this session's five topics did you find most relevant or helpful? Explain.

❏ Good Sex Doesn't Just Happen
❏ Untangling the "Nots" in Unhealthy Sex
❏ Keep the Home Fires Burning
❏ Unfaithfulness Is More than Just Adultery
❏ Facing Sexual Dysfunction

★ Share one or two insights from the text that you found especially encouraging.

_____

_____

_____

Which of the following lifelines will you grab this week? What specific step(s) will you take to help rescue yourself and thereby rescue your marriage?

❏ Give sex time and space so that it gets the attention it deserves. If you invest time in growing together and keep working on it, the returns will be worth it all.

❏ Work on your sex life in order to rebuild your connection.

❏ Become a student of good sex in marriage as well as a student of each other and yourself.

❏ A strong support group will help you remain faithful to your mate in every sense. If you already have such a group, use it! If you don't, this week take a step toward establishing one.

❏ Only love and safety can help a couple out of the performance trap and into what sex is meant to be: a deeper way of knowing each other. If you need help to get there, by all means, get that help.

_____

_____

As you close in prayer, ask the Lord to give you the strength to untangle the "nots" in unhealthy sex, courage to face sexual dysfunction, grace to offer your mate forgiveness if unfaithfulness is an issue, and creativity to overcome barriers to having time for each other. Ask God to help make your connection a place of love and safety so that sex can be the gift He intends it to be.

When you go to the meeting, be ready to . . .

• SHARE YOUR ANSWERS TO THE STARRED (★) QUESTIONS.

• CHOOSE WHICH OF THE LIFELINES YOU'LL GRAB AND WORK ON THIS WEEK.

During the week . . .

• AS YOU WORK ON YOUR SECTION 8 LIFELINE, PAY ATTENTION TO THE EFFECTS OF YOUR EFFORTS ON YOU, ON YOUR MATE, AND ON YOUR MARRIAGE.

Embark on a
Life-Changing Journey
of Personal and Spiritual Growth

DR. HENRY CLOUD   **DR. JOHN TOWNSEND**

Dr. Henry Cloud and Dr. John Townsend have been bringing hope and healing to millions for over two decades. They have helped people everywhere discover solutions to life's most difficult personal and relational challenges. Their material provides solid, practical answers and offers guidance in the areas of *parenting, singles issues, personal growth,* and *leadership.*

Bring either Dr. Cloud or Dr. Townsend to your church or organization. They are available for:

- Seminars on a wide variety of topics
- Training for small group leaders
- Conferences
- Educational events
- Consulting with your organization

Other opportunities to experience Dr. Cloud and Dr. Townsend:

- Ultimate Leadership workshops—held in Southern California throughout the year
- Small group curriculum
- Seminars via Satellite
- Solutions Audio Club—Solutions is a weekly recorded presentation

For other resources, and for dates of seminars and workshops
by Dr. Cloud and Dr. Townsend, visit:
www.cloudtownsend.com

For other information **Call (800) 676-HOPE (4673)**

Or write to:
Cloud-Townsend Resources
3176 Pullman Street, Suite 105
Costa Mesa, CA

DON'T YOU HATE IT WHEN YOU'VE DONE EVERYTHING YOU KNOW TO DO AND YOU STILL CAN'T MAKE IT WORK?

In *God Will Make a Way* and *What to Do When You Don't Know What to Do*, Dr. Henry Cloud and Dr. John Townsend present eight fascinating and persuasive principles that demonstrate how God moves in difficult situations. *God Will Make a Way* shows the principles at work in twelve key areas of life such as personal goals, sex, dating, conflict, parenting, fear, destructive habits and more. You'll have the tools you need to regain control of your life, make your relationships better, and satisfy your spiritual hunger.

Whether you're currently in a "fix" or just looking for more out of life, these books are about how God shows up in ways you never dreamed possible.

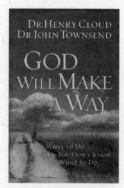

God Will Make a Way
1-59145-008-X

**God Will Make a Way
Personal Discovery Guide**
1-59145-079-9

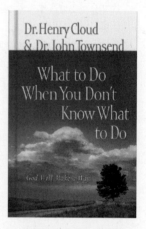

**What to Do When
You Don't Know What
to Do**
1-59145-153-1

AVAILABLE WHEREVER BOOKS ARE SOLD